STEVE MUDWAY

Alpha
AND
Omega

A SIMPLIFIED GUIDE
TO END DAYS PROPHECY

STEVE MUDWAY

Alpha AND Omega

A SIMPLIFIED GUIDE
TO END DAYS PROPHECY

MEREO
Cirencester

Mereo Books

1A The Wool Market Dyer Street Cirencester Gloucestershire GL7 2PR
An imprint of Memoirs Publishing www.mereobooks.com

Alpha and Omega: 978-1-86151-367-0

First published in Great Britain in 2014
by Mereo Books, an imprint of Memoirs Publishing

The address for Memoirs Publishing Group Limited can be found at
www.memoirspublishing.com

The Memoirs Publishing Group Ltd Reg. No. 7834348

The Memoirs Publishing Group supports both The Forest Stewardship Council® (FSC®) and
the PEFC® leading international forest-certification organisations. Our books carrying both the
FSC label and the PEFC® and are printed on FSC®-certified paper. FSC® is the only
forest-certification scheme supported by the leading environmental organisations including
Greenpeace. Our paper procurement policy can be found at
www.memoirspublishing.com/environment

Typeset in 11/15pt bembo
by Wiltshire Associates Publisher Services Ltd. Printed and bound in Great Britain by
Printondemand-Worldwide, Peterborough PE2 6XD

FOREWORD

It is a daunting prospect to consider writing about a subject as controversial as End Days Prophecy, if only because of the amount of study and research carried out already by those notable scholars who have gone before, as well as those of us who now live in the hope of the Lord's imminent return. There is a wealth of information freely available on the Internet, with some of it being truly excellent work, but sadly, much of it is totally absurd and misleading. How are we to tell the difference between what is sound teaching and what is not?

The only reliable answers must be found in the scriptures themselves, even if their truths are, at times, well and truly hidden. It is in the hope of encouraging others to look at this subject for themselves that I have set down my thoughts in writing, trusting that in the process, some light will be shed on questions previously unanswered. To delay much longer might have meant writing a history, rather than about prophecy, as all the signs indicate that we are in the last stages of this world's final struggle with itself, and against its own Creator.

I offer up my findings to anyone who cares to read them, in the hope that you will derive as much pleasure from considering these truths as I have. There is, of course, no obligation on your part to concur with anything written here, and whilst some of you may agree with my conclusions and find answers to difficult questions, others may think this is a wild departure from traditional thinking, and prefer one of the many other options available to them. I have tried to describe the process that has led to my present standpoint, but I realistically accept that some will just not agree with me. So be it!

I have aimed to be as accurate as I can be, but because of the length of time that has passed since Daniel and others wrote down what they were given, as well as the fact that history is notoriously fickle, there will be conflicts of opinion. Often in this field, the answer you get will depend on who you ask, so I make no claim here to have all the answers, and on the contrary, you may find this book will only serve to raise more questions for you.

I have worked methodically through scripture to give some background to the subject, explaining things as I go, hopefully in a straightforward manner. It is my firm belief that the scriptures were written with the ordinary man in mind, so that armed with a desire to know the truth, and prepared to put in some reasonable effort, anyone who approaches God for understanding should eventually be rewarded with a satisfactory explanation of what He has written to us in His Word. I hope to have made a complex subject as simple as possible by cutting through some of the theology that discourages many from even contemplating the study of End Day Prophecy, or eschatology as it is known by the grown-ups. Any treatment as short as this one is must assume a certain amount of biblical knowledge on the reader's part, so I apologize in advance if I expect a bit of homework from you, or presume that you are more familiar with the subject than you really are. If reading this book serves only to fire your interest in what the Lord's future appearances involve for both the Church and the nation Israel, I will consider that it was well worth writing.

Always in His Grace

Steve Mudway, Cropredy, 5th August 2014
alphaandomega70@hotmail.com

CONTENTS

NEBUCHADNEZZAR

❧

Nebuchadnezzar's Dream, Daniel 2:19-45:

Then was the secret revealed unto Daniel in a night vision. Then Daniel blessed the God of heaven. Daniel answered and said, Blessed be the name of God for ever and ever: for wisdom and might are His: And He changeth the times and the seasons: He removeth kings, and setteth up kings: He giveth wisdom unto the wise, and knowledge to them that know understanding: He revealeth the deep and secret things: He knoweth what is in the darkness, and the light dwelleth with Him. I thank Thee, and praise Thee, O Thou God of my fathers, Who hast given me wisdom and might, and hast made known unto me now what we desired of Thee: for Thou hast now made known unto us the king's matter. Therefore Daniel went in unto Arioch, whom the king had ordained to destroy the wise men of Babylon: he went and said thus unto him; Destroy not the wise men of Babylon: bring me in before the king, and I will shew unto the king the interpretation. Then Arioch brought in Daniel before the king in haste, and said thus unto him, I have found a man of the captives of Judah, that will make known unto the king the interpretation. The king answered and said to Daniel, whose name was Belteshazzar, Art thou able to make known unto me the dream which I have seen, and the interpretation thereof? Daniel answered in the presence of the king, and said, The secret which the king hath demanded cannot the wise men, the astrologers, the magicians, the soothsayers, shew unto the king; But there is a God in heaven that revealeth secrets, and maketh known to the king Nebuchadnezzar what shall be in the latter days. Thy dream, and the visions of thy head upon thy bed, are these; As for thee, O king, thy thoughts came into thy mind upon thy bed, what should come to pass hereafter: and He that revealeth secrets maketh known to thee what shall come to pass. But as for me, this secret is not revealed to me for any wisdom that I have more than any living, but for their sakes that shall make known the interpretation to the king, and that thou mightest know the thoughts of thy heart.

Thou, O king, sawest, and behold a great image. This great image, whose brightness was excellent, stood before thee; and the form thereof was terrible. This image's head was of fine gold, his breast and his arms of silver, his belly and his thighs of brass, His legs of iron, his feet part of iron and part of clay. Thou sawest till that a stone was cut out without hands, which smote the image upon his feet that were of iron and clay, and brake them to pieces. Then was the iron, the clay, the brass, the silver, and the gold, broken to pieces together, and became like the chaff of the summer threshingfloors; and the wind carried them away, that no place was found for them: and the stone that smote the image became a great mountain, and filled the whole earth. This is the dream; and we will tell the interpretation thereof before the king.

Thou, O king, art a king of kings: for the God of heaven hath given thee a kingdom, power, and strength, and glory. And wheresoever the children of men dwell, the beasts of the field and the fowls of the heaven hath He given into thine hand, and hath made thee ruler over them all. Thou art this head of gold. And after thee shall arise another kingdom inferior to thee, and another third kingdom of brass, which shall bear rule over all the earth. And the fourth kingdom shall be strong as iron: forasmuch as iron breaketh in pieces and subdueth all things: and as iron that breaketh all these, shall it break in pieces and bruise. And *whereas thou sawest the feet and toes, part of potters' clay, and part of iron, the kingdom shall be divided; but there shall be in it of the strength of the iron, forasmuch as thou sawest the iron mixed with miry clay. And as the toes of the feet were part of iron, and part of clay, so the kingdom shall be partly strong, and partly broken. And whereas thou sawest iron mixed with miry clay, they shall mingle themselves with the seed of men: but they shall not cleave one to another, even as iron is not mixed with clay. And in the days of these kings shall the God of heaven set up a kingdom, which shall never be destroyed: and the kingdom shall not be left to other people, but it shall break in pieces and consume all these kingdoms, and it shall stand for ever. Forasmuch as thou sawest that the stone was cut out of the mountain without hands, and that it brake in pieces the iron, the brass, the clay, the silver, and the gold; the great God hath made known to the king what shall come to pass hereafter: and the dream is certain, and the interpretation thereof sure.*

Daniel's story is well known, and any further study of his experiences would be well rewarded, but our interest here is regarding prophecy of the end times, a subject in which Daniel was shown only a [1]limited part. Daniel and his companions were known to the king to be 'ten times better' than the other wise men, Daniel himself being able to give interpretations on visions and dreams. But when the king had his dream, it did not occur to him to go straight to Daniel. He went instead to the Chaldeans. These were a distinct class of the Babylonians, reputed experts in dreams, astrology and learning generally. They were Daniel's teachers, so it should be no surprise that they kept Daniel and his friends out of it, perhaps because of their professional jealousy. When they had failed to give the king the answer, they further provoked him by saying he was asking the

1. Daniel 12: 8-9.

3

impossible, and so inevitably the order went out for all the wise men to be killed. Daniel had to go to the king in order to save himself and his companions, and was then given time to find the answer. When speaking to the king, he wisely confined himself to giving the credit to the "God in heaven that revealeth secrets" and both the dream and the interpretation were given to him.

It is simple enough in its basic form. The king dreamed about an image, clearly in a man's form but made out of various metals, head of gold, chest and arms of silver, belly and thighs of brass and legs and toes of iron. Additionally, the feet and toes are mixed with clay. He then saw the image destroyed by a stone 'cut out without hands' which hit the image in the feet, and shattered the whole thing, until it was just dust.

The interpretation shows that Nebuchadnezzar himself is represented by the head, and that his kingdom, the Babylonian empire had been given him by God. Then follow after this three other kingdoms, the Persian, Greek and Roman, represented respectively in the silver, brass and iron. What we have is a prophecy that shows the progression of time, these being the successive empires that were to rule over the Middle East, and elsewhere. This is now a matter of fact historically, and is undisputed. However, these empires, or a representative form of them, must exist together when they are destroyed by the stone, for the weakness seen in the feet, where it is struck, causes the rest of the image to be turned to dust, the 'chaff of the summer threshing-floors' which is blown away by the wind.

The image therefore represents both a succession in time, that which has already occurred, and a situation, at its end, where all nations represented in the image can be seen together, which to date has not yet happened. From Daniel's standpoint, of course, all of this was yet future.

The kingdoms are numbered one to four, but there is a distinction made between the legs of iron, and the feet and toes. The strength of this last part of the image is reduced because it is not completely metal but includes potter's clay, presumably baked, which is strong but brittle, and inclined to shatter. This is explained to Daniel, who writes "they shall mingle themselves with the seed of men, but they shall not cleave one to another, even as iron is not mixed with clay". This provides a clue to the image itself, as it is evident from the interpretation that the clay part is the seed of men, so the metal parts must be something else. This can only mean that the power and strength of the image, and the empires it represents, are not due to man, but to spiritual beings. God Himself takes the credit for giving Nebuchadnezzar his empire, and proves His power over it later by both taking it away from him, and then restoring it to him again. God Himself has the final power, but it is evident that angels are fighting battles in the heavens regarding the [2]control of nations, and this must be what is represented by this image. It looks as if it describes the kingdoms of men and their efforts to get control, but in reality it mirrors a power struggle in heaven for the control over the earth. The purity and value represented in the gold, is diminished as the other empires succeed it, until finally the purity is restored with the setting up of the final kingdom, the Stone, which is God's Everlasting Kingdom.

In the final end of the image, men become involved, but not in the sense of being one with the spiritual beings, for the two do not [3]mix. What is described is rather the involvement of men with the heavenly powers that are controlling these nations. The clay is also included with the other metals in the destruction of the image, so it does merit consideration in its own right. This

2. See Daniel 10:12-14.

of course is at the end time, and so is more than likely represented by the ten toes in the image.

There is one other aspect to consider here, for Nebuchadnezzar's dream clearly covers the time from his own period until the very end, when the stone destroys all previous traces of the kingdoms. However, the Babylonian Empire was not the first to dominate the Middle East, or more specifically Jerusalem. Before Babylon came first the Egyptian, then the Assyrian Empires. It may help to list them in order: Egyptian, Assyrian, Babylon, Persian, Greek, Roman and following Rome, the legs and the feet, which could well be regarded as the Ottoman Empire, ie Turkey. The Roman Empire never completely finished in the way the others did, but was divided into the Western and Eastern Empires with separate emperors. Constantine, who converted to Christianity, moved the empire's capital from Rome to Byzantium around 324AD, and named it Constantinople, which would later become the [4]Byzantine Empire, then later still, the Ottoman Empire.

This last empire was dismantled at the conclusion of the First World War in 1918, because of Turkey's alliance with Germany, which itself lost the war to the British and their allies. Following this, there was a movement to establish the principal of forming a separate [5]state of Israel, a homeland for the Jews. However, it was not until 1948, after the Second World War had ended, that the Jewish State of Israel became a reality. It should be seen therefore that we are still in the period of the end of the 'legs and the feet' in prophetic terms, for while the Roman Empire in its previous greatness has long gone, the final destruction typified in the 'stone' has not yet appeared.

3. There were angels who came to earth, and took the daughters of men as recorded in Genesis 6:1-2, but they had to take a physical form to do this. Their offspring became the 'giants' such as Goliath, and his sons. Daniel's account shows that this is not the case here, but rather man's involvement with the powers of heaven.

4. Constantinople, was first called Byzantium, later becoming Istanbul.

5. See the 'Balfour agreement' for more detail.

Daniel's companions walking in the fire:

Daniel 3:8-13: *Wherefore at that time certain Chaldeans came near, and accused the Jews. They spake and said to the king Nebuchadnezzar, O king, live forever. Thou, O king, hast made a decree, that every man that shall hear the sound of the cornet, flute, harp, sackbut, psaltery, and dulcimer, and all kinds of musick, shall fall down and worship the golden image: And whoso falleth not down and worshippeth, that he should be cast into the midst of a burning fiery furnace. There are certain Jews whom thou hast set over the affairs of the province of Babylon, Shadrach, Meshach, and Abed-nego; these men, O king, have not regarded thee: they serve not thy gods, nor worship the golden image which thou hast set up. Then Nebuchadnezzar in his rage and fury commanded to bring Shadrach, Meshach, and Abednego. Then they brought these men before the king.*

Daniel is not mentioned in the account of the fiery furnace, but as he was set up as a governor of Babylon and master of the magicians, it would not be prudent for the Chaldeans to try and bring any open accusation against him. Possibly envious because of their embarrassment in the matter of Nebuchadnezzar's dream, they seek to find an excuse to undermine Daniel's supporters, and feel confident enough to bring this matter to the king. It is not absolutely clear what this image was, or why it was set up, but it has been suggested that it was an edifice to Nebuchadnezzar, probably after a success in battle, and so a refusal to bow before it would constitute a direct insult to him. On this occasion the faithful are delivered, but in the later account in the Book of Revelation, a refusal to bow before the future image of the time, the abomination of desolation, results in death. There is no reason to believe that the golden image here is an exact model for the later image of Revelation, as the dimensions given are not consistent with any statue, or image of man. However, this does give an example of how unscrupulous men will use any device to manipulate situations for their own purposes, and this could well be the pattern of things to come in the latter times, particularly for Israel.

Nebuchadnezzar's madness:

Daniel 4:8-17: *But at the last Daniel came in before me, whose name was Belteshazzar, according to the name of my god, and in whom is the spirit of the holy gods: and before him I told the dream, saying, O Belteshazzar, master of the magicians, because I know that the spirit of the holy gods is in thee, and no secret troubleth thee, tell me the visions of my dream that I have seen, and the interpretation thereof. Thus were the visions of mine head in my bed; I saw, and behold a tree in the midst of the earth, and the height thereof was great. The tree grew, and was strong, and the height thereof reached unto heaven, and the sight thereof to the end of all the earth: The leaves thereof were fair, and the fruit thereof much, and in it was meat for all: the beasts of the field had shadow under it, and the fowls of the heaven dwelt in the boughs thereof, and all flesh was fed of it. I saw in the visions of my head upon my bed, and, behold, a watcher and an holy one came down from heaven; He cried aloud, and said thus, Hew down the tree, and cut off his branches, shake off his leaves, and scatter his fruit: let the beasts get away from under it, and the fowls from his branches: Nevertheless leave the stump of his roots in the earth, even with a band of iron and brass, in the tender grass of the field; and let it be wet with the dew of heaven, and let his portion be with the beasts in the grass of the earth: Let his heart be changed from man's, and let a beast's heart be given unto him; and let seven times pass over him. This matter is by the decree of the watchers,*

and the demand by the word of the holy ones: to the intent that the living
may know that the Most High ruleth in the kingdom of men, and giveth
it to whomsoever he will, and setteth up over it the basest of men.

Once again, Daniel seems to be the last one called to interpret
the dream, and only after other avenues are exhausted does the
king involve him. This may be a reflection on the king's view
of Daniel, influenced by the Chaldeans, but could equally show
the levels of bureaucracy involved in the court, where there is
a set order of advisors, with certain protocols to be observed.
Such delays only serve to prevent the immediate fulfilment of
God's will; they will never stop it happening. In fact, we should
recognize that in the scriptures any such delays are always under
God's overall control, and often serve His purpose exactly,
where the prophetic calendar is concerned. Here the dream
involves Nebuchadnezzar, and serves as a warning to him to
consider his ways.

This time a 'watcher or a [6]'holy one' delivers the message,
which has been decreed by more 'watchers'. Clearly these are
heavenly beings whose role it is to keep an eye on events on
earth, and having power to act if certain breaches occur, or when
set boundaries are crossed. In this case it is Nebuchadnezzar
himself, who in making claims above his station, is quickly
brought back to reality. He needed to appreciate that his power
came from God, and not his own strength or abilities! Rarely is
such divine intervention exercised; yet it does exist. More often
than not, events are allowed to take their natural course, but the
fact remains that this world is still accountable to God, Who in
His own time and His own way, will take control.

6. Angel, saint or guardian.

Belshazzar's Feast, and the end of the Babylonian Empire,:

Daniel 5:18-31: *O thou king, the Most High God gave Nebuchadnezzar thy father a kingdom, and majesty, and glory, and honour: And for the majesty that He gave him, all people, nations, and languages, trembled and feared before him: whom he would he slew; and whom he would he kept alive; and whom he would he set up; and whom he would he put down. But when his heart was lifted up, and his mind hardened in pride, he was deposed from his kingly throne, and they took his glory from him: And he was driven from the sons of men; and his heart was made like the beasts, and his dwelling was with the wild asses: they fed him with grass like oxen, and his body was wet with the dew of heaven; till he knew that the Most High God ruled in the kingdom of men, and that He appointeth over it whomsoever He will. And thou his son, O Belshazzar, hast not humbled thine heart, though thou knewest all this; But hast lifted up thyself against the Lord of heaven; and they have brought the vessels of his house before thee, and thou, and thy lords, thy wives, and thy concubines, have drunk wine in them; and thou hast praised the gods of silver, and gold, of brass, iron, wood, and stone, which see not, nor hear, nor know: and the God in Whose hand thy breath is, and Whose are all thy ways, hast thou not glorified: Then was the part of the hand sent from him; and this writing was written. And this is the writing that was written, MENE, MENE, TEKEL, UPHARSIN. This is the interpretation of the thing: MENE; God hath numbered thy kingdom, and finished it. TEKEL; Thou art weighed in the balances, and art found wanting. PERES; Thy kingdom is divided, and given to the Medes and Persians. Then commanded Belshazzar, and they clothed Daniel with scarlet, and put a chain of gold about his neck, and made a proclamation concerning him, that he should be the third ruler in the kingdom. In that night was Belshazzar the king of the Chaldeans slain. And Darius the Median took the kingdom, being about threescore and two years old."*

Belshazzar was the grandson of Nebuchadnezzar, but had no knowledge of Daniel, who was probably enjoying retirement at this time. Daniel had no qualms about explaining to Belshazzar the facts of life, before translating what could be clearly seen written on the wall. To his credit, Belshazzar accepts Daniel's words and promotes him as promised, but this is short lived, as that very night, Belshazzar is killed, the kingdom changes hands and the Medes take control. It is said that this was an internal betrayal, and that the Median army led by the general Gobryas went up a through a dried-up riverbed to gain control of the city. The victory is credited to 'Darius the Mede' but as no figure of that name exists in history [7]the historians' assertion that Astyages was the king referred to at the [8]time is probably the correct one. The names Darius and Cyrus occur several times in the line of the Mede and Persian kings.

Daniel, who by then was already an old man, finds himself with a new king to serve, and is quickly promoted in the kingdom. Again, there is an attempt to discredit him in the king's eyes, and his refusal to change his practice of worship, after the king's decree gives the excuse to his contemporaries, those 'certain men of the presidents and princes' to accuse him to the king. He is then thrown into the den of lions, because they tricked the king. Daniel of course is saved on this occasion, and apart from the destruction of the accusers of Daniel, along with their families, the only result is that once again the 'God of Daniel, the living God' is to be feared in the empire by decree of the king. Here is another example of how men, provoked by their jealousy, can be used to try the righteous, with the underlying intention of removing them out of God's purpose.

7. As the word 'Darius' is a title meaning 'restrainer/maintainer' also used by other kings.
8. See also Isaiah 45:1.

If Daniel had died here, then we would not have had the later writings from him that form the basis of God's Prophetic message. Daniel however, prospered even to the reign of the Persian king Cyrus.

CHAPTER TWO

DANIEL'S VISIONS

The next two chapters of Daniel refer to dreams and visions given him before the Babylonian kingdom ended:

Daniel 7:1-28: *In the first year of Belshazzar king of Babylon Daniel had a dream and visions of his head upon his bed: then he wrote the dream, and told the sum of the matters. Daniel spake and said, I saw in my vision by night, and, behold, the four winds of the heaven strove upon the great sea. And four great beasts came up from the sea, diverse one from another. The first was like a lion, and had eagle's wings: I beheld till the wings thereof were plucked, and it was lifted up from the earth, and made stand upon the feet as a man, and a man's heart was given to it. And behold another beast, a second, like to a bear, and it raised up itself on one side, and it had three ribs in the mouth of it between the teeth of it: and they said thus unto it, Arise, devour much flesh. After this I beheld, and lo another, like a leopard, which had upon the back of it four wings of a fowl; the beast had also four heads; and dominion was given to it. After this I saw in the night visions, and behold a fourth beast, dreadful and terrible, and strong exceedingly; and it had great iron teeth: it devoured and brake in pieces, and stamped the residue with the feet of it: and it was diverse from all the beasts that were before it; and it had ten horns. I considered the horns, and, behold, there came up among them another little horn, before whom there were three of the first horns plucked up by the roots: and, behold, in this horn were eyes* like the eyes of man, and a mouth speaking great things. I beheld till the thrones were cast down, and the Ancient of Days did sit, Whose garment was white as snow, and the hair of His head like the pure wool: His throne was like the fiery flame, and His wheels as burning fire. A fiery stream issued and came forth from before Him: thousand thousands ministered unto Him, and ten thousand times ten thousand stood before Him: the judgment was set, and the books were opened. I beheld then because of the voice of the great words which the horn spake: I beheld even till the beast was slain, and his body destroyed, and given to the burning flame.

As concerning the rest of the beasts, they had their dominion taken away: yet their lives were prolonged for a season and time. I saw in the night visions, and, behold, one like the Son of Man came with the clouds of heaven, and came to the Ancient of Days, and they brought Him near before Him. And there was given Him dominion, and glory, and a kingdom, that all people, nations, and languages, should serve Him: His dominion is an everlasting dominion, which shall not pass away, and His kingdom that which shall not be destroyed. I Daniel was grieved in my spirit in the midst of my body, and the visions of my head troubled me. I came near unto one of them that stood by, and asked him the truth of all this. So he told me, and made me know the interpretation of the things. These great beasts, which are four, are four kings, which shall arise out of the earth. But the saints of the Most High shall take the kingdom, and possess the kingdom for ever, even for ever and ever.

Then I would know the truth of the fourth beast, which was diverse from all the others, exceeding dreadful, whose teeth were of iron, and his nails of brass; which devoured, brake in pieces, and stamped the residue with his feet; And of the ten horns that were in his head, and of the other which came up, and before whom three fell; even of that horn that had eyes, and a mouth that spake very great things, whose look was more stout than his fellows. I beheld, and the same horn made war with *the saints, and prevailed against them; Until the Ancient of Days came, and judgment was given to the saints of the Most High; and the time came that the saints possessed the kingdom. Thus he said, The fourth beast shall be the fourth kingdom upon earth, which shall be diverse from all kingdoms, and shall devour the whole earth, and shall tread it down, and break it in pieces. And the ten horns out of this kingdom are ten kings that shall arise: and another shall rise after them; and he shall be diverse from the first, and he shall subdue three kings. And he shall speak great words against the Most High, and shall wear out the saints of the Most High, and think to change times and laws: and they shall be given into his hand until a time and times and the dividing of time. But the judgment shall sit, and they shall take away his dominion, to consume and to destroy it unto the end. And the kingdom and dominion, and the greatness of the kingdom under the whole heaven, shall be given to the people of the saints of the Most High, Whose kingdom is an everlasting kingdom, and all dominions shall serve and obey Him. Hitherto is the end of the matter. As for me Daniel, my cogitations much troubled me, and my countenance changed in me: but I kept the matter in my heart.*

This dream is given to Daniel himself, and contains both similarities and differences when compared to the earlier one given to Nebuchadnezzar. We should be careful to differentiate between what was given to Daniel and what was shown to Nebuchadnezzar, for if we make assumptions here we could lose the truths given. The four great beasts in this account appear after the four winds strive on the great sea, the [9]Mediterranean. Four beasts arrive, one after the other, but then exist together. This marks a difference, as the image of Nebuchadnezzar's dream

9. There have been two world wars that have directly affected the balance of power in the Mediterranean area, and led to the forming of the nation Israel.

denotes a succession in time, but these kingdoms are clearly future to Daniel, exist together, and relate to the end times. Here they are described as animals, rather than sections of a man, and are only indirectly related to the first image. We seem to be led rather to their animal characteristics, for they are 'like' a lion etc, but clearly no lion or leopard has wings, and ribs don't talk! They represent aspects of the former kingdoms, but do not correspond exactly to the earlier four kingdoms, or Empires, of Nebuchadnezzar's dream.

In the first, the lion with its wings plucked, we see the beast with the feet of a man and with a man's heart, and therefore with a man's limited and fleshly outlook. The second, the bear, is raised on one side, and is carrying three ribs in its mouth that appear to have some control over it. This is odd, but there is no explanation given here to Daniel. The third, the leopard with fowl's wings, receives dominion, and the fourth is described as differing from the others: "it devoured and brake in pieces, and stamped the residue with the feet of it: and it was diverse from all the beasts that were before it; and it had ten horns".

Clearly the fourth beast [10]dominates the other three, the residue (= the rest/others), however it does not destroy them, for they continue even after the fourth beast is dealt with. Daniel's interest is drawn immediately to the fourth beast, which implies that he understood the nature of the first three, although they were still future to him.

It might be interesting to note that there are only two occasions where lions, bears and leopards are associated together in scripture, (apart from being described as beasts in dreams such as Daniel's). The first is Hosea 13:6-9:

10. Compare this beast with the one appearing in Revelation 13:1-2, where the characteristics of the previous beasts are now combined in the one.

According to their pasture, so were they filled; they were filled, and their heart was exalted; therefore have they forgotten Me. Therefore I will be unto them as a lion: as a leopard by the way will I observe them: I will meet them as a bear that is [11]bereaved of her whelps, and will rend the caul of their heart, and there will I devour them like a lion: the wild beast shall tear them. O Israel, thou hast destroyed thyself; but in Me is thine help.

Here the Lord describes these animals as instruments of His judgment on Israel. Then follows Isaiah 11:1-9:

And there shall come forth a rod out of the stem of Jesse, and a Branch shall grow out of his roots: And the spirit of the Lord shall rest upon Him, the spirit of wisdom and understanding, the spirit of counsel and might, the spirit of knowledge and of the fear of the Lord; And shall make Him of quick understanding in the fear of the Lord: and He shall not judge after the sight of His eyes, neither reprove after the hearing of His ears: But with righteousness shall He judge the poor, and reprove with equity for the meek of the earth: and He shall smite the earth with the rod of His mouth, and with the breath of His lips shall He slay the wicked. And righteousness shall be the girdle of His loins, and faithfulness the girdle of His reins. The wolf also shall dwell with the lamb, and the leopard shall lie down with the kid; and the calf and the young lion and the fatling together; and a little child shall lead them. And the cow and the bear shall feed; their young ones shall lie down together: and the lion shall eat straw like the ox. And the sucking child shall play on the hole of the asp, and the weaned child shall put his hand on the cockatrice' den. They shall not hurt nor destroy in all My holy mountain: for the earth shall be full of the knowledge of the Lord, as the waters cover the sea.

11. Does this explain the three ribs in the bear's mouth? Is it a cry for revenge from the bear's whelps? Is this nation aggrieved against Israel for some real or imagined loss? A pre-emptive strike could take place, for example, and this could cause their ranging about, seeking revenge or recompense? The bear is not a known symbol of Iran, although the ram and lion were used at some points.

Here the description is of the Lord's future rule, and of a world reconciled to Him. In the light of this, it might be better to regard these beasts that arise from the sea as individual nations, representing the empires that they once were, but reduced in size and influence. Although significant in their own right, they become subservient to the fourth beast almost as soon as it appears. These would now be modern-day Iraq (Babylonian), Iran (Persian/Mede), Greece (or more likely Syria, representing Greece through the line of the Seleucid kings) and Turkey (representing Rome as the Eastern Empire) but their significance is in their role as the nations that will be used to judge and try Israel in the last days, rather than in their former glory as Empires.

Returning to the narrative, Daniel's interest is drawn to the fourth of these beasts, clearly more ferocious and ambitious than the others. Questioning reveals that the beast has ten horns, and that there is another horn that appears from elsewhere to then dominate three of the 'kings' or horns. Through these three he gains control of the other seven, and determines, with their assent, to make war with the saints, and thus overcome Israel. It is after this period that he, and the ten are destroyed.

Note his methods:

Daniel 7:25: *And he shall speak great words against the Most High, and shall wear out the saints of the Most High, and think to change times and laws.*

This 'horn' is remarkable for his words, and this is one way that he differs from the others. Although he eventually resorts to military means to gain power, his initial rise is by the clever use of words, at first insinuating himself into three horns, then into the remaining seven. Remarkable, because he is clearly not one of them, but hails from somewhere else. His power over Israel is restricted to a defined period:

Daniel 7:25-26: ...*and they shall be given into his hand until a time and times and the dividing of time. But the judgment shall sit, and they shall take away his dominion, to consume and to destroy it unto the end.*

His end comes after completely overcoming Israel, after which the Lord resumes control, and raises up His newly reconciled people, Israel. Attempts to confine this prophecy to any historical fulfilment ignore the fact that these kingdoms must all be present at this end time, but then become absorbed into the fourth kingdom of the 'little horn', the 'horn', or the 'Beast'. Daniel's question concerns this man, who continues in his blasphemous words even as his judgment is being set up. He is certainly a force to be reckoned with, as much for his convincing rhetoric, as his eventual military power and influence. Daniel's second vision follows two years later:

Daniel 8:1-27: *In the third year of the reign of king Belshazzar a vision appeared unto me, even unto me Daniel, after that which appeared unto me at the first. And I saw in a vision; and it came to pass, when I saw, that I was at Shushan in the palace, which is in the province of Elam; and I saw in a vision, and I was by the river of Ulai. Then I lifted up mine eyes, and saw, and, behold, there stood before the river a ram which had two horns: and the two horns were high; but one was higher than the other, and the higher came up last. I saw the ram pushing westward, and northward, and southward; so that no beasts might stand before him, neither was there any that could deliver out of his hand; but he did according to his will, and became great. And as I was considering, behold, an he goat came from the west on the face of the whole earth, and touched not the ground: and the goat had a notable horn between his eyes. And he came to the ram that had two horns, which I had seen standing before the river, and ran unto him in the fury of his power. And I saw him come close unto the ram, and he was moved with choler against him, and smote the ram, and brake his two horns: and there was no power in the ram to stand before him, but he cast him down to the ground, and stamped upon him: and there was none that could deliver the ram out of his hand. Therefore the he goat waxed very great: and when he was strong, the great horn was broken; and for it came up four notable ones toward the four winds of heaven. And out of one of them came forth a little horn, which waxed exceeding great, toward the south, and toward the east, and toward the pleasant land. And it waxed great, even to the host of heaven; and it cast down some of the host and of the stars to the ground, and stamped upon them. Yea, he magnified himself even to the prince of the host, and by him the daily sacrifice was taken away, and the place of his sanctuary was cast down. And an host was given him against the daily sacrifice by reason of transgression, and it cast down the truth to the ground; and it practiced, and prospered. Then I heard one saint speaking, and another saint said unto that certain saint which spake, How long shall be the vision concerning the daily sacrifice, and the transgression of desolation, to give both the sanctuary and the host to be trodden under foot? And he said unto me, unto two thousand and three hundred days; then shall the sanctuary be cleansed.*

And it came to pass, when I, even I Daniel, had seen the vision, and sought for the meaning, then, behold, there stood before me as the appearance of a man. And I heard a man's voice between the banks of Ulai, which called, and said, Gabriel, make this man to understand the vision. So he came near where I stood: and when he came, I was afraid, and fell upon my face: but he said unto me, Understand, O son of man: for at the time of the end shall be the vision. Now as he was speaking with me, I was in a deep sleep on my face toward the ground: but he touched me, and set me upright. And he said, Behold, I will make thee know what shall be in the last end of the indignation: for at the time appointed the end shall be. The ram which thou sawest having two horns are the kings of Media and Persia. And the rough goat is the king of Grecia: and the great horn that is between his eyes is the first king. Now that being broken, whereas four stood up for it, four kingdoms shall stand up out of the nation, but not in his power. And in the latter time of their kingdom, when the transgressors are come to the full, a king of fierce countenance, and understanding dark sentences, shall stand up. And his power shall be mighty, but not by his own power: and he shall destroy wonderfully, and shall prosper, and practise, and shall destroy the mighty and the holy people. And through his policy also he shall cause craft to prosper in his hand; and he shall magnify himself in his heart, and by peace shall destroy many: he shall also stand up against the Prince of princes; but he shall be broken without hand. And the vision of the evening and the morning which was told is true: wherefore shut thou up the vision; for it shall be for many days. And I Daniel fainted, and was sick certain days; afterward I rose up, and did the king's business; and I was astonished at the vision, but none understood it."

Two years after the first vision comes a second, and this time there is no mystery about who the nations involved are, as they are identified both by name and emblem, the Greeks being the 'He goat' and the Medes and Persians the 'Ram'. The high, and the higher horns of the Ram equate to the Medes and Persians, and the 'notable horn' of the he-goat is Alexander the Great. On Alexander's death, the horn becomes the four notable horns, as the Greek Empire is sub-divided into four areas, roughly equivalent to the present borders of Greece, Turkey, Syria and Egypt. Daniel's second vision is given as a revelation of what is about to happen after the Babylonian Empire is taken over by the Medes, for at the time of this vision, Babylon is yet to be toppled. However the scope of this prophecy extends far beyond the days of the successive empires, for after Daniel had sought for understanding, he is told:

Daniel 8: 17-19: *Understand, O son of man: for at the time of the end shall be the vision. Now as he was speaking with me, I was in a deep sleep on my face toward the ground: but he touched me, and set me upright. And he said, Behold, I will make thee know what shall be in the last end of the indignation: for at the time appointed the end shall be.*

This revelation follows the pattern of the previous two, for some of the events relate to Daniel's time and the four successive empires, but then it also extends to the time of the end, when these nations appear together, albeit with a reduced sphere of influence. We can see that the visions are progressive, and information is being added as we go along. We know that the 'little horn' appears within a group of three of the ten horns of the former Roman Empire, but we also know that he is not from them. Here we have more information concerning his origins, for he is clearly now associated with one of the four divisions of the Greek Empire. Further, we learn that he "waxed great towards the South, the East, and the pleasant land," so he is unlikely to originate from any of them.

There is a character who appears later in history who may well serve as a type of the latter day 'horn'; he is named as Antiochus IV Epiphanes, a Seleucid (Greek/Syrian) king, who invaded south into Egypt. He returned to Jerusalem in fury, after an [12]uprising, and was responsible for the slaughter of thousands

---

12. The result of a rumour of his death, and internal struggles within Jerusalem The Maccabean revolt of 167 BC, under Judas Maccabee followed after these atrocities and the sack of the temple, committed by him. The period between the desecration of the altar, and its cleansing was three and a half years.

of Jews, as well as the desecration of the temple site. He tried to outlaw Jewish worship, and produced coins that promoted his own deity. From a historical point of view, he was then a likely candidate to be the 'horn', but this vision extends beyond any historical fulfilment to the time of the end, which means that there is yet another man to come who must fulfil these prophecies and will be destroyed prior to the Lord's kingdom being established. There is more detail to be considered here, for the little horn has more far reaching plans than just the control of Israel:

Daniel 8:10-14: *And it waxed great, even to the host of heaven; and it cast down some of the host and of the stars to the ground, and stamped upon them. Yea, he magnified himself even to the prince of the host, and by him the daily sacrifice was taken away, and the place of his sanctuary was cast down. And an host was given him against the daily sacrifice by reason of transgression, and it cast down the truth to the ground; and it practiced, and prospered. Then I heard one saint speaking, and another saint said unto that certain saint which spake, How long shall be the vision concerning the daily sacrifice, and the transgression of desolation, to give both the sanctuary and the host to be trodden under foot? And he said unto me, unto two thousand and three hundred days; then shall the sanctuary be cleansed.*

Eventually the ambition of the 'little horn' causes him to seek to interfere with the worship of Israel, extending his challenge to the 'host of heaven'. The fact that he takes away the daily sacrifice presents a difficulty here, for at present there is no 'daily sacrifice' for Israel, as this can only take place on the historic site of the temple, known as the dome of the rock. This is a sacred Muslim site, from which Mohammed is said to have risen to heaven. The present situation is that Jews can access the site, but are physically prevented from having any form of gathering or prayer there. Clearly, some changes must occur, and this must be the subject of the covenant that is to be made with Israel, spoken of in Daniel 9:27. From the narrative, it seems a transgression takes place, giving the 'horn' the excuse to invade Israel, and that for a period given as [13]two thousand and three hundred days, he is allowed to dominate Israel, after which time the sanctuary is cleansed once again, and worship restored.

In order for this to happen Israel must have an agreement concerning the reinstatement of its daily sacrifice, and at some point three and a half years into the agreement there is a breach or a change made, causing a rift between Israel and the horn. This results in a full-scale invasion. Note the words given in the angel's explanation:

Daniel 8:23-25: *And in the latter time of their kingdom, when the transgressors are come to the full, a king of fierce countenance, and understanding dark sentences, shall stand up. And his power shall be mighty, but not by his own power: and he shall destroy wonderfully, and shall prosper, and practise, and shall destroy the mighty and the holy people. And through his policy also he shall cause craft to prosper in his hand; and he shall magnify himself in his heart, and by peace shall destroy many: he shall also stand up against the Prince of princes; but he shall be broken without hand.*

His method to begin with is deception, he destroys with 'peace' (an agreement?) and yet here his power comes from elsewhere. He 'understands dark sentences, craft prospers in his hand, and

---

13. Where times are so specific, we must accept they are valid, so this period, working on the prophetic month of thirty days, is equivalent to six years and four months. More properly translated 'evening and mornings', to equate to the two daily sacrifices. (This could mean that the time is halved.)

he shall 'magnify himself in his heart, and shall stand up against the prince of princes' before he is destroyed. Compare this with Daniel's previous vision:

Daniel 7:25: *And he shall speak great words against the Most High, and shall wear out the saints of the Most High, and think to change times and laws: and they shall be given into his hand until a time and times and the dividing of time.*

Here we see that he will "think to change times and laws." A possible scenario is that the rift will come about when, having established the agreement, he tries to change the conditions regarding the sacrifice, which in turn could provoke a revolt from the believing Jews of this time, as previously occurred in the days of Antiochus Epiphanes. This character, the horn, emerges as a peacemaker who deceives others by his grandiose and commendable speeches before his real character is revealed. He is involved with [14]demonic power, and insinuates himself into a position of authority by his good words and speeches.

What better way to convince the world of his good intentions than to broker a deal between Arab and Jew, and so help to bring all of the Middle Eastern nations together? He is certainly very plausible in his beginning, and tells the world what it wants to hear. Fortunately, his time in power is restricted, and his end is certain. What is also certain is that when he does overrun Israel, they are in for a very unpleasant time!

---

14. This is where the clay, of the toes/feet can be seen.

CHAPTER THREE

THE SEVENTY YEARS OF JEREMIAH

Daniel 9:1-3: *In the first year of Darius the son of Ahasuerus, of the seed of the Medes, which was made king over the realm of the Chaldeans; In the first year of his reign I Daniel understood by books the number of the years, whereof the Word of the Lord came to Jeremiah the prophet, that He would accomplish seventy years in the desolations of Jerusalem. And I set my face unto the Lord God, to seek by prayer and supplications, with fasting, and sackcloth, and ashes.*

Here we see Daniel's effort to understand the periods of captivity for his people, the Jews, at Babylon. His concern was for the restoration of his people to their own land, and even more so as he had been in Babylon for sixty-eight years by then, and must have been wondering if he would ever return. We should be clear that there are three periods that need to be understood regarding these times, and they are the [15]Servitude the [16]Captivity, and the [17]Desolations. As it stood, Daniel could expect to be in Babylon for a further ten years, to complete both the Servitude and Captivity periods. However, it is not that simple.

To explain this: it was because of the initial Jewish refusal to

15. 606 BC Daniel and his friends are taken to Babylon.
16. 598 BC Jeconiah taken to Babylon.
17. 589 BC When Israel is invaded by Nebuchadnezzar.

be subject to Babylonian rule under Nebuchadnezzar that the situation worsened, until eventually all but the poorest people were removed into exile. Daniel was taken at the beginning of the first period, the Servitude, but the Captivity began eight years later, stated to be for seventy years from its beginning to its end. The period of the Desolations began nine years after that, and it is this period that Daniel was considering from Jeremiah's writings.

Jeremiah 29:10-14: *For thus saith the Lord, That after seventy years be accomplished at Babylon I will visit you, and perform My good word toward you, in causing you to return to this place. For I know the thoughts that I think toward you, saith the Lord, thoughts of peace, and not of evil, to give you an expected end. Then shall ye call upon Me, and ye shall go and pray unto Me, and I will hearken unto you. And ye shall seek Me, and find Me, when ye shall search for Me with all your heart. And I will be found of you, saith the Lord: and I will turn away your captivity, and I will gather you from all the nations, and from all the places whither I have driven you, saith the Lord; and I will bring you again into the place whence I caused you to be carried away captive.*

Daniel's supplication and prayer are timely however, because within two years, the people are allowed to return, effectively [18]shortening the period to make it seventy years from the Servitude, rather than from the Captivity. Notice that in Daniel's supplication for his people he included himself, and his words were clearly a response to Jeremiah's words, for the people to seek the Lord, Who will then give deliverance from Babylon. Is it possible that Daniel's prayer caused the Lord to change His mind and allow the people to return earlier?

18. 536BC, The Decree of Cyrus, which authorised the Jewish return to Jerusalem (ends both the Servitude & Captivity).

Daniel must have suspected that there was more to this than just the three periods of subjection to Babylon, as he continued to pray and offer his supplications. Because of his continued interest, Gabriel was sent to clear up any misunderstanding, and to give Daniel 'skill and understanding'. What follows is an explanation of the prophecy of the Desolations period, with implications for Israel that Daniel was previously unaware of.

Daniel 9:20-27: *And while I was speaking, and praying, and confessing my sin and the sin of my people Israel, and presenting my supplication before the Lord my God for the holy mountain of my God; Yea, whiles I was speaking in prayer, even the man Gabriel, whom I had seen in the vision at the beginning, being caused to fly swiftly, touched me about the time of the evening oblation. And he informed me, and talked with me, and said, O Daniel, I am now come forth to give thee skill and understanding. At the beginning of thy supplications the commandment came forth, and I am come to shew thee; for thou art greatly beloved: therefore understand the matter, and consider the vision. Seventy weeks are determined upon thy people and upon thy holy city, to finish the transgression, and to make an end of sins, and to make reconciliation for iniquity, and to bring in everlasting righteousness, and to seal up the vision and prophecy, and to anoint the Most Holy. Know therefore and understand, that from the going forth of the commandment to restore and to build Jerusalem unto the Messiah the Prince shall be seven weeks, and threescore and two weeks: the street shall be built again, and the wall, even in troublous times. And after threescore and two weeks shall Messiah be cut off, but not for Himself: and the people of the prince that shall come shall destroy the city and the sanctuary; and the end thereof shall be with a flood, and unto the end of the war desolations are determined. And he shall confirm the covenant with many for one week: and in the midst of the week he shall cause the sacrifice and the oblation*

to cease, and for the overspreading of abominations he shall make it
desolate, even until the consummation, and that determined shall be
poured upon the desolate.

This explanation given to Daniel, but not previously revealed in Jeremiah's writings, shows that there is a further period of Desolations not yet commenced, which will consist of seventy weeks and extend to the 'end', which is the final setting up of God's kingdom. Sixty-nine of the weeks begin at the commandment to rebuild Jerusalem and end at the cutting off of Messiah, which is the crucifixion of the Lord in Jerusalem. There is a [19]further 'week' after this to make up the seventy. This, of course, is not a period of 'years' only, but as the Hebrew word for week (*shebuah*, meaning a period of sevens) means seven, a whole period of 70 x 7 years = 490 years is represented.

This took Daniel's understanding of what is involved for his people to an entirely new level, which was, of course, related to his previous visions concerning the 'four kingdoms' and the 'little horn', the Beast himself. Daniel had been given a definitive timescale, and a specific starting point for this new seventy-year period of 490 years. Jewish blessing then was not just about going back into the land and the restoration of its temple worship, but extended to the Messiah's coming, his cutting off and the final confrontation between the Beast and the Lord's people, Israel.

This period of seventy weeks is broken into three distinct periods of seven, sixty-two, and one. This gives periods of: forty-nine, four hundred and thirty-four and seven years respectively. The commandment to build the temple came in 445BC, and

---

19. Which involves two halves, based around a covenant of seven years regarding the daily sacrifice, made by the 'prince that shall come'. This is broken mid-week, after three and a half years. The remaining three and a half years involve the final desolation of Israel, the great tribulation that the Lord spoke of.

forty-nine years after this, in 397 BC, the Hebrew canon of scripture was completed with the book of Malachi. A further four hundred and thirty-four years will bring us to the Lord's death on the cross, [20]32 AD.

The final week is yet to come, and cannot be accounted for by any historical event. This final period of seven years is identified by the angel as being relevant to the reinstatement of the evening and morning daily sacrifice, and is a still future event. It could be said that this final week is not consecutive with the other periods as it does not follow from the Lord's death, but Sir Robert Anderson accounts for this in his superb book *The Coming Prince*. To explain this briefly: the Jews themselves accept that their prophetic history is not counted during periods of apostasy, when they were, in effect, cut off from God's will. This was the case after the Lord's crucifixion and resurrection, when despite the ministry of Paul and the other apostles, the Jews once again rejected Him. There is yet a period of seven years during which the Jewish nation will start to seek for their Messiah, and at the beginning of this the prophetic clock will start ticking again for the nation.

Daniel's final vision

It is a popular practice amongst some scholars to dismiss the book of Daniel as a work of history by implying that it was written long after the events described in it and attributing some parts of it to authors other than Daniel. The view held here is that both the book of Daniel and its author are genuine, and such difficulties that are contained in it can either be resolved

---

20. These calculations have been treated in far more depth in Sir Robert Anderson's excellent book 'The Coming Prince'. It is hoped here only to give an overview of what is involved.

by comparison with other scriptures, or by accepting that God will make His truth known in the fullness of time. Daniel had many questions himself, to which he was not given answers.

One of the difficulties when we study Daniel is that he wrote both of events of his own time and of events that were future and prophetic. Some of these prophecies have now been fulfilled, and are indeed a matter of history yet there remain many events written in the book that are yet to be seen, and are clearly reserved for the 'end times', so we cannot regard the book as closed in any way, because of partial historical fulfilments. The passages we are now to consider come into both categories, for there are some historical fulfilments of these events, but a yet future part remains to be completed.

For the historical part, what we have described is the transition of Empires from the Persian to the Greek, and then into the early part of the Roman.

Daniel 10:1-21: *In the third year of Cyrus king of Persia a thing was revealed unto Daniel, whose name was called Belteshazzar; and the thing was true, but the time appointed was long: and he understood the thing, and had understanding of the vision. In those days I Daniel was mourning three full weeks. I ate no pleasant bread, neither came flesh nor wine in my mouth, neither did I anoint myself at all, till three whole weeks were fulfilled. And in the four and twentieth day of the first month, as I was by the side of the great river, which is Hiddekel; Then I lifted up mine eyes, and looked, and behold a certain man clothed in linen, whose loins were girded with fine gold of Uphaz: His body also was like the beryl, and his face as the appearance of lightning, and his eyes as lamps of fire, and his arms and his feet like in colour to polished brass, and the voice of his words like the voice of a multitude. And I Daniel alone saw the vision: for the men that were with me saw not the vision; but a great quaking fell upon them, so that they fled to hide themselves. Therefore I was left alone, and saw this great vision, and there remained no strength in me: for my comeliness was turned in me into corruption, and I retained no strength. Yet heard I the voice of his words: and when I heard the voice of his words, then was I in a deep sleep on my face, and my face toward the ground. And, behold, an hand touched me, which set me upon my knees and upon the palms of my hands. And he said unto me, O Daniel, a man greatly beloved, understand the words that I speak unto thee, and stand upright: for unto thee am I now sent. And when he had spoken this word unto me, I stood trembling. Then said he unto me, Fear not, Daniel: for from the first day that thou didst set thine heart to understand, and to chasten thyself before thy God, thy words were heard, and I am come for thy words. But the prince of the kingdom of Persia withstood me one and twenty days: but, lo, Michael, one of the chief princes, came to help me; and I remained there with the kings of Persia. Now I am come to make thee understand what shall befall thy people in the latter days: for yet the vision is for many days.*

And when he had spoken such words unto me, I set my face toward the ground, and I became dumb. And, behold, one like the similitude of the sons of men touched my lips: then I opened my mouth, and spake, and said unto him that stood before me, O my lord, by the vision my sorrows are turned upon me, and I have retained no strength. For how can the servant of this my lord talk with this my lord? for as for me, straightway there remained no strength in me, neither is there breath left in me. Then there came again and touched me one like the appearance of a man, and he strengthened me, And said, O man greatly beloved, fear not: peace be unto thee, be strong, yea, be strong. And when he had spoken unto me, I was strengthened, and said, Let my lord speak; for thou hast strengthened me. Then said he, Knowest thou wherefore I come unto thee? and now will I return to fight with the prince of Persia:

and when I am gone forth, lo, the prince of Grecia shall come. But I will shew thee that which is noted in the scripture of truth: and there is none that holdeth with me in these things, but Michael your prince.

There are some questions in Daniel's mind, for he presents himself to the Lord for more understanding. The three weeks that he has been praying coincide with the twenty-one days that this angel has been in conflict with the Prince of Persia, and when this battle is finished, the angel says the 'Prince of Grecia shall come'. We can conclude that the passing of these empires from one to another is a matter decided in the spiritual sphere, and greatly contested, so that even the revealing of these things to men (such as Daniel) is the subject of spiritual opposition in high places. Daniel was heard straight away, but other angels prevented this particular angel from coming to him with the news.

Daniel 11:1-45: *Also I in the first year of Darius the Mede, even I, stood to confirm and to strengthen him. And now will I shew thee the truth. Behold, there shall stand up yet three kings in Persia; and the fourth shall be far richer than they all: and by his strength through his riches he shall stir up all against the realm of Grecia. And a mighty king shall stand up, that shall rule with great dominion, and do according to his will. And when he shall stand up, his kingdom shall be broken, and shall be divided toward the four winds of heaven; and not to his posterity, nor according to his dominion which he ruled: for his kingdom shall be plucked up, even for others beside those.*

And the king of the south shall be strong, and one of his princes; and he shall be strong above him, and have dominion; his dominion shall be a great dominion. And in the end of years they shall join themselves together; for the king's daughter of the south shall come to the king of the north to make an agreement: but she shall not retain the power of the arm; neither shall he stand, nor his arm: but she shall be given up, and they that brought her, and he that begat her, and he that strengthened her in these times. But out of a branch of her roots shall one stand up in his estate, which shall come with an army, and shall enter into the fortress of the king of the north, and shall deal against them, and shall prevail: And shall also carry captives into Egypt their gods, with their princes, and with their precious vessels of silver and of gold; and he shall continue more years than the king of the north. So the king of the south shall come into his kingdom, and shall return into his own land. But his sons shall be stirred up, and shall assemble a multitude of great forces: and one shall certainly come, and overflow, and pass through: then shall he return, and be stirred up, even to his fortress. And the king of the south shall be moved with choler, and shall come forth and fight with him, even with the king of the north: and he shall set forth a great multitude; but the multitude shall be given into his hand. And when he hath taken away the multitude, his heart shall be lifted up; and he shall cast down many ten thousands: but he shall not be strengthened by it.

For the king of the north shall return, and shall set forth a multitude greater than the former, and shall certainly come after certain years with a great army and with much riches. And in those times there shall many stand up against the king of the south: also the robbers of thy people shall exalt themselves to establish the vision; but they shall fall. So the king of the north shall come, and cast up a mount, and take the most fenced cities: and the arms of the south shall not withstand, neither his chosen people, neither shall there be any strength to withstand. But he that cometh against him shall do according to his own will, and none shall stand before him: and he shall stand in the glorious land, which by his hand shall be consumed. He shall also set his face to enter with the strength of his whole kingdom, and upright ones with him; thus shall he do: and he shall give him the daughter of women, corrupting her: but she shall not stand on his side, neither be for him. After this shall he turn his face unto the isles, and shall take many: but a prince for his own behalf shall cause the reproach offered by him to cease; without his own reproach he shall cause it to turn upon him. Then he shall turn his face toward the fort of his own land: but he shall stumble and fall, and not be found. Then shall stand up in his estate a raiser of taxes in the glory of the kingdom: but within few days he shall be destroyed, neither in anger, nor in battle.

And in his estate shall stand up a vile person, to whom they shall not give the honour of the kingdom: but he shall come in peaceably, and obtain the kingdom by flatteries. And with the arms of a flood shall they be overflown from before him, and shall be broken; yea, also the prince of the covenant. And after the league made with him he shall work deceitfully: for he shall come up, and shall become strong with a small people. He shall enter peaceably even upon the fattest places of the province; and he shall do that which his fathers have not done, nor his fathers' fathers; he shall scatter among them the prey, and spoil, and riches: yea, and he shall forecast his devices against the strong holds, even for a time. And he shall stir up his power and his courage against the king of the south with a great army; and the king of the south shall be stirred up to battle with a very great and mighty army; but he shall not stand: for they shall forecast devices against him. Yea, they that feed of the portion of his meat shall destroy him, and his army shall overflow: and many shall fall down slain. And both these kings' hearts shall be to do mischief, and they shall speak lies at one table; but it shall not prosper: for yet the end shall be at the time appointed. Then shall he return into his land with great riches; and his heart shall be against the holy covenant; and he shall do exploits, and return to his own land. At the time appointed he shall return, and come toward the south; but it shall not be as the former, or as the latter.

Daniel is being shown the succession of power from his own time to that of the Greeks under Alexander, the division of his empire into four and the comings and goings of the kings of the North, who are the Seleucid kings, and the kings of the South, who are the Ptolemys. An attempt is later made to join these two kingdoms with the marriage of Bernice, the daughter of the king of the South, to the then present king of the North. However, our interest is drawn to the 'vile person' who comes in peaceably and takes the kingdom. He is the aforementioned Antiochus IV Epiphanes, who exhibits many of the characteristics of the 'little horn' who is to follow. At this time, his intention is to overrun Egypt, passing through Israel on the way. Once in Egypt, he finds himself challenged by the 'ships of Chittim' (islands, or coastal regions), commonly understood to mean Cyprus, but more accurately referring to the [21]Romans. In his fury, he returns to Jerusalem and sacks the city, desecrating the temple by slaughtering pigs on the altar and setting up a statue to Zeus, the King of the Greek gods:

Daniel 11:30-32: *For the ships of Chittim shall come against him: therefore he shall be grieved, and return, and have indignation against the holy covenant: so shall he do; he shall even return, and have intelligence with them that forsake the holy covenant. And arms shall stand on his part, and they shall pollute the sanctuary of strength, and shall take away the daily sacrifice, and they shall place the abomination that maketh desolate. And such as do wickedly against the covenant shall he corrupt by flatteries: but the people that do know their God shall be strong, and do exploits.*

---

21. As interpreted in the Septuagint, the translation into Greek of the Old Testament, produced for Hellenized Jews.

It is at this time that we depart from any historical fulfilment, for Antiochus died four years later and therefore cannot be the king who fulfils the rest of the account. After he desecrated the temple, there was a rebellion against his intention to Hellenize the Jews by Matthias, and the Maccabean revolt began. The temple was then rededicated, and the sacrifices resumed. The account turns to the Jews again, and seems to apply to them for the remainder of the prophecy, up to the 'end'. This represents accurately the history of the Jews to the present day:

Daniel 11:33-35: *And they that understand among the people shall instruct many: yet they shall fall by the sword, and by flame, by captivity, and by spoil, many days. Now when they shall fall, they shall be holpen with a little help: but many shall cleave to them with flatteries. And some of them of understanding shall fall, to try them, and to purge, and to make them white, even to the time of the end: because it is yet for a time appointed.*

The king that now appears is a different one to Antiochus Epiphanes, and there is no direct evidence to say where he comes from. However, because his reign follows from the Seleucid line, it is an indication that he comes from the same area, now modern Syria, and that his reign is yet future to us

Daniel 11:36-45: *And the king shall do according to his will; and he shall exalt himself, and magnify himself above every god, and shall speak marvellous things against the God of gods, and shall prosper till the indignation be accomplished: for that that is determined shall be done. Neither shall he regard the God of his fathers, nor the desire of women, nor regard any god: for he shall magnify himself above all. But in his estate shall he honour the god of forces: and a god whom his fathers knew not shall he honour with gold, and silver, and with precious stones, and pleasant things. Thus shall he do in the most strong holds with a strange god, whom he shall acknowledge and increase with glory: and he shall cause them to rule over many, and shall divide the land for gain. And at the time of the end shall the king of the south push at him: and the king of the north shall come against him like a whirlwind, with chariots, and with horsemen, and with many ships; and he shall enter into the countries, and shall overflow and pass over. He shall enter also into the glorious land, and many countries shall be overthrown: but these shall escape out of his hand, even Edom, and Moab, and the chief of the children of Ammon. He shall stretch forth his hand also upon the countries: and the land of Egypt shall not escape. But he shall have power over the treasures of gold and of silver, and over all the precious things of Egypt: and the Libyans and the Ethiopians shall be at his steps. But tidings out of the east and out of the north shall trouble him: therefore he shall go forth with great fury to destroy, and utterly to make away many. And he shall plant the tabernacles of his palace between the seas in the glorious holy mountain; yet he shall come to his end, and none shall help him.*

The antagonism between these two nations, Syria and Egypt, seems to reappear at the time of the end, and the 'horn' in his effort to invade Egypt passes through Israel and other counties. For reasons not given, Edom, Moab and Ammon, countries roughly equivalent to modern-day Jordan, escape his attention. This is probably where the believing Jews will flee in the later times of persecution.

Daniel 12:1: *And at that time shall Michael stand up, the great prince which standeth for the children of thy people: and there shall be a time of trouble, such as never was since there was a nation even to that same time: and at that time thy people shall be delivered, every one that shall be found written in the book.*

These last verses can clearly be identified as the 'great tribulation' of which the Lord spoke. This is ominous, as this persecution of the Jews will surpass that of the holocaust and every previous effort to wipe out the Jewish nation.

Daniel 12:2-3: *And many of them that sleep in the dust of the earth shall awake, some to everlasting life, and some to shame and everlasting contempt. And they that be wise shall shine as the brightness of the firmament; and they that turn many to righteousness as the stars for ever and ever.*

What is evident is that through the ministry of the wise at this time, many of the Jews shall be turned to righteousness, even in this time of great trouble. Daniel was not given any further details; he had done his work in recording the visions and understanding given to him, but further knowledge of what these events entailed was reserved for others near the time of the end. There is however, some more tantalizing information to come from the two angels, and it concerns the timings involved in this final week.

Daniel 12:4-13: *But thou, O Daniel, shut up the words, and seal the book, even to the time of the end: many shall run to and fro, and knowledge shall be increased. Then I Daniel looked, and, behold, there stood other two, the one on this side of the bank of the river, and the other on that side of the bank of the river. And one said to the man clothed in linen, which was upon the waters of the river, How long shall it be to the end of these wonders? And I heard the man clothed in linen, which was upon the waters of the river, when he held up his right hand and his left hand unto heaven, and sware by Him that liveth for ever that it shall be for a time, times, and an half; and when he shall have accomplished to scatter the power of the holy people, all these things shall be finished. And I heard, but I understood not: then said I, O my Lord, what shall be the end of these things? And he said, Go thy way, Daniel: for the words are closed up and sealed till the time of the end. Many shall be purified, and made white, and tried; but the wicked shall do wickedly: and none of the wicked shall understand; but the wise shall understand. And from the time that the daily sacrifice shall be taken away, and the abomination that maketh desolate set up, there shall be a thousand two hundred and ninety days. Blessed is he that waiteth, and cometh to the thousand three hundred and five and thirty days. But go thou thy way till the end be: for thou shalt rest, and stand in thy lot at the end of the days.*

The times, times and a half, readily equate to the three and a half years, or 1260 days, of the second half of the final week, which is stated in Revelation. However, there are two other periods mentioned in this passage, one of two thousand three hundred and ninety days (30 days longer than the Revelation period of 1260 days,) and another period of one thousand three hundred and thirty-five days, when the blessing shall be on those that wait. From these times, there is a period of first thirty, then forty-five days after the finish of the last week, before the final blessing is given to Israel. There is no explanation of this given here, but in due course this period can be examined.

In conclusion then, the book of Daniel is given to us as a framework, the straight edges of the jigsaw puzzle that is end day prophecy, into which we can place further revelations, given throughout the scriptures. It shows that the development of prophetic utterance can involve both the near and far future, and is elastic enough to cover great periods of time, and also accommodate change before coming to its final fulfilment. It will all be found to be true in the end, but remains flexible enough to allow men to change their minds, and choose whether to accept or deny the truth. For example: when the Lord came, it would have been possible for Israel as a nation to accept Him, and then events might have been hastened, or accomplished, in a different way. As it was, His people chose first to reject Him, then the ministry of the apostles, and finally the ministry of Paul. Therefore, the final week of the seventy is yet to commence.

The agreement with a country, or several countries, brokered by an individual, in regards to the Jewish temple worship for the duration of seven years, is the only certain indication of the commencement of the last prophetic week for Israel. This is yet future to us, but even now some Jews are making preparation for their daily sacrifice to be reinstated, and we can be sure that world events, particularly in the Middle East, are conspiring to bring Daniel's dreams and visions nearer to fruition. He was clearly loved by the Lord, and his earthly reward was in the revelation he was given of future events concerning his own nation, in the will of God. His interest in these things, and his earnest efforts to find out more, brought forth his book, which is a foundation for our further study.

CHAPTER FOUR

THE LORD AND PROPHECY

❀

When considering the Lord's words concerning the end times, it is essential to recognise that everything He talked about concerned His own nation, Israel. Attempts to read the Gentile church into His teachings will just present confusion. Whilst He always accepted that Gentiles, or non-Jews, had a place in His Father's will, He also understood that His own ministry was to the Jewish people and His discourses on the end days were confined to what they needed to know for their own spiritual blessing and survival. He spoke more than once on these things, usually in response to the disciples' curiosity about His teachings, and from what they already knew from the prophetic writings that had gone before. The Church as we know it, did not exist at this time, being a mystery not revealed until later, when Paul spoke about it, following the Jewish rejection of their Saviour. For the purpose of clarity, we will consider both the Jewish and Gentile church experience separately, and so the Lord's words should be read as referring only to the nation Israel, telling them what they need to be aware of. The records of the Lord's teachings on the end days are contained in the Gospels of Matthew, Mark, and Luke. John's contribution comes later when he writes the Book of Revelation, and he, like Daniel, was rewarded with a special understanding of what was to take place.

Matthew contains more detail than the other two Gospels, so we shall consider it first:

Matthew 24:1-3: *And Jesus went out, and departed from the temple: and His disciples came to Him for to shew Him the buildings of the temple. And Jesus said unto them, See ye not all these things? verily I say unto you, There shall not be left here one stone upon another, that shall not be thrown down. And as He sat upon the mount of Olives, the disciples came unto Him privately, saying, Tell us, when shall these things be? and what shall be the sign of Thy coming, and of the end of the world?*

The disciples' questioning about the end days follows from the Lord's answer to them concerning the temple. He responds to their enthusiasm concerning the temple buildings with the sombre warning that 'there shall not be one stone left upon another', and so His views on religious buildings, and this one in particular, are made clear from the start. They mean nothing to Him!

This throws the disciples out somewhat, and once they had thought about it, they question Him with 'When shall these things be, what shall be the sign of Thy coming, and of the end of the world'? Their questions give Him the opportunity to start to teach about the real sequence of events. Regarding the temple, we know that its destruction was in 70AD by the Romans, but this was not what His answer to them is about. He doesn't want to confuse them here[22], and talks to them about the second part of their question, showing them how they would know that all of these things were about to take place.

22. The destruction of the temple signalled the end of the Jewish nation for the time being, and did not mark the commencement either of the tribulation, or the last seven weeks. The last temple was Herod's, and not significant in God's plan. The time of its destruction may have had some bearing on events if the Jews had accepted the apostles teaching concerning the kingdom, but we cannot be certain of that.

Matthew 24:4-5: *And Jesus answered and said unto them, Take heed that no man deceive you. For many shall come in My name, saying, I am Christ; and shall deceive many.*

The truly interesting thing here is that the Lord warns of 'many' coming in His name, claiming to be the Christ. We know from Daniel's writings that there is one in particular, the Beast, who will make that eventual claim, and the Lord was fully aware of him, but never refers to him except in the collective sense of his being included as one of the many. The fact is that being deceived is a distinct possibility for the Jews in the end times, and whether they are deceived by the ultimate fraud, the Beast, or by one of the lesser ones, it makes no difference. The warning is that there will be 'many' who make the claim, and not one of them is to be believed.

Matthew 24:6: *And ye shall hear of wars and rumours of wars: see that ye be not troubled: for all these things must come to pass, but the end is not yet.*

Another sign of the end times for Israel is the 'wars, and rumours of wars.' Wars are not new of course, but if we look at the Middle East, and in particular the area around Israel, then all we hear about is wars, and the rumour of them. It is an extremely turbulent area, where violence between countries or within countries is commonplace. From the Jewish point of view, their country is surrounded by hostile groups, both political and religious, many of these with the stated aim of wiping Israel off the map. If ever these various factions manage to unite against Israel, they would be a real threat to its security.

Matthew 24:7: *For nation shall rise against nation, and kingdom against kingdom.*

Amazingly, the Jewish believer is not to be troubled by these things! We have to put this in perspective; they are bound to be troubled, of course, and the wars are the signs of things to come, but not *the* particular sign that the disciples are looking for. Likewise, in Matthew 24:7-8: ...*and there shall be famines, and pestilences, and earthquakes, in divers places. All these are the beginning of sorrows.*

Famines are one of the side effects of wars or natural disasters, and tend to affect people's focus. It is easy in these situations for blame and dissent to arise, and any leadership can quickly gain a following if it seems to have an answer, or a solution. Hitler, for example, traded on the economic uncertainty of 1930s Germany to eventually promote himself to high office. The Lord is not saying that these disasters are of no account, but is pointing to their relative importance as signs of the end. He calls them the beginning of sorrows, correctly translated as the birth pangs, increasing in frequency and intensity, leading up to the greater sorrows that are to come for the nation.

Matthew 24:9-10: *Then shall they deliver you up to be afflicted, and shall kill you: and ye shall be hated of all nations for My name's sake. And then shall many be offended, and shall betray one another, and shall hate one another.*

These verses show an escalation of hostilities when the Jews themselves are persecuted and hated by all nations. This would suggest that there is a focus again on their nation, as God's people as a spiritual force rather than the political state it now is, and the love of many for their Lord will then be tested. This is by both the resurgence of false teachers and the internal betrayal of differing factions. The emphasis then will be on endurance and holding fast to the true teaching that will be available, whilst patiently waiting for the Lord's appearance.

We have to consider Israel's emergence as the people of God once more, in the light of the prophecies of Daniel. We are looking at the beginnings of the seventieth week, the last seven years in the prophetic calendar that precede Israel's establishment as God's people. This commences with the signing of a seven-year treaty that includes an agreement for them to offer the daily sacrifice on the temple mount site. At present, this would mean some form of agreement with Jordan and the Palestinian Authority, and any negotiation about a peace deal may eventually have to include this as part of a comprehensive peace offer. Some compromises will have to be made on both sides, for it is a very emotive issue at this time. Not only will the Gospel of the kingdom then be preached in Israel, it will have far-reaching effects, in stirring up the latent hatred towards the Jewish nation that has always existed near the surface. Of course, the real teaching is opposed by false teaching, which the Lord once again warns about:

Matthew 24:11-14: *And many false prophets shall rise, and shall deceive many. And because iniquity shall abound, the love of many shall wax cold. But he that shall endure unto the end, the same shall be saved. And this gospel of the kingdom shall be preached in all the world for a witness unto all nations; and then shall the end come.*

We must remember from Daniel's writings that the seventy weeks, as a whole, is the total period of God's judgments on Israel, and refers to the Gentile domination of its lands before the Lord's blessing, and the fulfilment of His promise takes effect.

Sixty-nine of these weeks have been fulfilled already and since the time of Malachi's prophecy, Israel has been waiting for the final week to fulfil this period. John the Baptist could have been the herald of these days, and the Lord's appearing after him could then have been the catalyst for Israel to takes its place amongst the nations, as the Lord's chosen people on earth. But it was not to be, for they would not accept their Lord, nor the later witness of the apostles. This resulted, at the end of the Acts period, in the Lord declaring the 'mystery of the church' as preached by Paul, being a body of believers who were initially Jewish, but over time consisted predominantly of Christian Gentile converts.

The Church is a people taken out of all nations who believe the Lord's teachings about Himself, and that collectively have a special place in the will of God. There is a fullness of this people: a certain number who are to be brought into the Christian Church within a certain timescale, before all are caught up to heaven. The ministry and witness of the Lord will then return to the Jewish nation, as His people on earth. The timing of this is not altogether clear, and there could be a transition period where the Church remains on earth, and yet the Jewish ministry begins, with its daily sacrifice having been established. This seven-year deal starts the prophetic clock ticking again for Israel, and includes the events now described by the Lord. It is punctuated, in its middle, by the following sign:

Matthew 24:15-21: *When ye therefore shall see the abomination of desolation, spoken of by Daniel the prophet, stand in the holy place, (whoso readeth, let him understand:) Then let them which be in Judaea flee into the mountains. Let him which is on the housetop not come down to take any thing out of his house: Neither let him which is in the field return back to take his clothes. And woe unto them that are with child, and to them that give suck in those days! But pray ye that your flight be not in the winter, neither on the sabbath day: For then shall be great tribulation, such as was not since the beginning of the world to this time, no, nor ever shall be.*

This describes the period of 'great tribulation' as opposed to the 'beginning of sorrows' that precedes it. This period of 'great tribulation' lasts for three and a half years, and at its end will conclude the seventy weeks that Daniel was shown written in the book of Jeremiah.

When we consider the gravity of the Lord's words here, we can see that any persecution of the Jews to date is but a foretaste of the hatred that will be unleashed upon them at this end time. The only sensible option for them is to leave, and there is a place prepared for this, '[23]the mountains'. This is one 'sign of the end' that the disciples had asked for: the 'abomination of desolation, spoken of by Daniel the prophet'. In this, the Lord endorses the prophecies of Daniel, and ties up the various visions that were given to him. We therefore need have no problem with Daniel being the author and recipient of revelation concerning these days, regardless of the various charges that have been brought against his writings by [24]subsequent scholars. The Lord accepted His writings.

Matthew 24:22-26: *And except those days should be shortened, there should no flesh be saved: but for the elect's sake those days shall be*

---

23. Probably in modern-day Jordan, for this nation seems to escape the influence of the Beast (Daniel 11:41). There are two seismic fault lines that converge in the Dead Sea area. The Carmel is a horizontal fault going through the Mount of Olives and the 'Great Rift' goes from Syria down through Israel, and then on through Saudi and Ethiopia. Another major earthquake is expected in Israel, the last one being in 1927, as they occur at approximately eighty-year intervals. Israelis will escape through the gap created by the split in the Mount of Olives, after an earthquake (Zechariah 14:4).

24. There have been several attacks made on his authorship, citing confusion over the languages used, and whether these were later writings etc. This alone should point us to the importance of the work, for if this foundation can be shaken, the whole of biblical prophecy can be put in question. The Lord's endorsement is all we need.

shortened. Then if any man shall say unto you, Lo, here is Christ, or there; believe it not. For there shall arise false Christs, and false prophets, and shall shew great signs and wonders; insomuch that, if it were possible, they shall deceive the very elect. Behold, I have told you before. Wherefore if they shall say unto you, Behold, He is in the desert; go not forth: behold, He is in the secret chambers; believe it not.

The persecution of these times is limited to the three and a half years, for should it continue longer, the whole nation would be wiped out. Again we see a warning against false Christs, and also false prophets. Previously the Lord warned of false Christs coming in at the 'beginnings of sorrows', and then false prophets who counteract the teachings of the kingdom. But now, after the abomination of desolation is set up (and we do not know what this is exactly, except that it replaces the daily sacrifice), there are both false Christs and false Prophets being mentioned together, who provide evidence for their claims by miraculous signs. This is a cruel test to those who are waiting for a sign from the Lord Himself and waiting for His deliverance from this widespread destruction, but these deceivers are not to be [25]believed. The sign of the Lord's appearing for the nation, when it comes, will be unmistakable:

Matthew 24:27-28: *For as the lightning cometh out of the east, and shineth even unto the west; so shall also the coming of the Son of Man be. For wheresoever the carcase is, there will the eagles be gathered together.*

25. It is of note that the Lord talks of 'many', whereas Daniel, and John in Revelation, talk of the one Beast (although he has many names, the beast, little horn etc), and the False Prophet. The Lord's warnings are to the Jews of the time, not the Church, who are not looking elsewhere for deliverance, and have found their Lord already.

The great tribulation of the three and a half years is now over, but the Lord does not immediately appear for His people. This may explain the differences in the various times given in scripture, for we know the number of the days as one thousand two hundred and sixty, or three and a half years, from John in Revelation. We also have a period of twelve hundred and ninety days from the end of Daniel, and another period of thirteen hundred and thirty-five. This gives a total of seventy-five days, from the end of the great tribulation, that the Jewish believer is required to wait. One explanation could be that there is a month where nothing apparently happens, and then:

Matthew 24:29-30: *Immediately after the tribulation of those days shall the sun be darkened, and the moon shall not give her light, and the stars shall fall from heaven, and the powers of the heavens shall be shaken: And then shall appear the sign of the Son of Man in heaven: and then shall all the tribes of the earth mourn, and they shall see the Son of Man coming in the clouds of heaven with power and great glory.*

This may account for the further 45-day period that the Jews are expected to wait, and is in itself a frightening experience, particularly for the world, which is now awaiting judgment for its non-belief, its lack of action to help the Jews, or perhaps even giving support to the persecutors of the nation Israel in its time of need. This is the final sign of the Lord's coming that the disciples had requested, but we do not know what it is. It is unlikely to be a cross, which although the most obvious and recognizable sign is also the symbol of the Lord's humiliation. Scripture suggests that it is the brightness of His coming that will be seen, so a great light is more likely to be the sign, which will be set in contrast to the previous darkness shrouding the earth.

Matthew 24:31 *And He shall send His angels with a great sound of a trumpet, and they shall gather together His elect from the four winds, from one end of heaven to the other.*

It is at this time that the elect, the believing Jews, are brought together in Israel, in anticipation of the blessing that is to come for having survived the period of God's judgements. The Lord's people will finally be in their own place, and from this time are set up as rulers of the Earth in His name. The Lord's teachings regarding the end do not finish here, and the following verses should be noted as part of the whole narrative:

Matthew 24:32-36: *Now learn a parable of the fig tree; When his branch is yet tender, and putteth forth leaves, ye know that summer is nigh: So likewise ye, when ye shall see all these things, know that it is near, even at the doors. Verily I say unto you, This generation shall not pass, till all these things be fulfilled. Heaven and earth shall pass away, but My words shall not pass away. But of that day and hour knoweth no man, no, not the angels of heaven, but My Father only.*

The people are to take the signs as an indication of the nearness of His coming, for when 'all these things' are visible, the generation that sees them begin will most likely see their end. The fact remains that the day and hour are hidden, known only by the Father, but the signs are given to show the nation the closeness of the coming, and allow them to prepare themselves. The line of descent of the Jews will not be broken; they will surely be present to the end, despite the past and future efforts of many to wipe them out completely. Again, we should apply these passages to the Lord's coming for the Jews, and not in any way to His coming for the Church.

Matthew 24:37-42: But as the days of Noe were, so shall also the coming of the Son of Man be. For as in the days that were before the flood they were eating and drinking, marrying and giving in marriage, until the day that Noe entered into the ark, And knew not until the flood came, and took them all away; so shall also the coming of the Son of Man be. Then shall two be in the field; the one shall be taken, and the other left. Two women shall be grinding at the mill; the one shall be taken, and the other left. Watch therefore: for ye know not what hour your Lord doth come.

This gives a further indication of the state of things prior to the Lord's appearing in His judgment on the earth, for the picture given is of the days of Noah, where eating, drinking and marriage preparations are the main concerns of the time. These are normal pastimes, and show the careless attitude of the people even in the face of the current and impending disasters. They are unconcerned about anything except their immediate lifestyle, and believe that things are going to continue in the same way forever.

Peter described Noah as a 'preacher of righteousness'. That suggests not only that he built the ark but that he told others why he was doing it, and what was about to happen. Their response to him was ridicule, and the same response is likely to be found in the end, for the attitude is the same:

2 Peter 3:3-7: *Knowing this first, that there shall come in the last days scoffers, walking after their own lusts, And saying, Where is the promise of His coming? For since the fathers fell asleep, all things continue as they were from the beginning of the creation. For this they willingly are ignorant of, that by the Word of God the heavens were of old, and the earth standing out of the water and in the water: Whereby the world*

that then was, being overflowed with water, perished: But the heavens and the earth, which are now, by the same Word are kept in store, reserved unto fire against the day of judgment and perdition of ungodly men.

For the Jew, ridiculing such teaching means a wilful neglect of their scriptures, for they are told by the Lord to be ready.

We should not confuse these days with what is written for the Church. The fact that the Lord describes two being in the field and one taken does not mean that the Jewish people will be mysteriously taken up, or raptured, as the Church will be. This is spoken of as being in the context of Noah's time, when some were aware of what was coming and others were not. When the time comes, the faithful will take warning and run, whereas the indifferent will continue with whatever they are doing. The whole context of the Lord's teaching to Israel is to be aware of the times. If they were to be taken up anyway and delivered, what would be the point of their having to run away to avoid the persecution?

Matthew 24:43-44: *But know this, that if the goodman of the house had known in what watch the thief would come, he would have watched, and would not have suffered his house to be broken up. Therefore be ye also ready: for in such an hour as ye think not the Son of Man cometh.*

The Lord's people, the nation Israel, are expected to be waiting for Him, and if they are doing this they will not be deceived and robbed of their blessing. The Lord's coming for the Jewish nation is as a thief in the night, and for those that are not ready, and therefore don't care, there is going to be loss. The Lord expects faithfulness from His people, and will be looking for faith when He comes. Each has his own responsibility as a servant, and if any individual is found neglecting his duty to God, it will be required of him.

Interestingly, the reference to drinking is taken up later as a theme common to both the Jewish and Gentile churches' end day experience, and the increase in drunkenness in recent years can be taken as an indicator of the impending end days. There is no quicker way to lose one's spiritual awareness than to become involved in excessive drinking or drug use, and the warnings in scripture are plain, particularly in relation to the end times. At the very least, it will sap your time and take away your spiritual perception, but being a very demanding mistress, it also leads into all sorts of barren involvement with non-believers, and in extreme, can take your life. Just say no!

Matthew 24:45-51: *Who then is a faithful and wise servant, whom his lord hath made ruler over his household, to give them meat in due season? Blessed is that servant, whom his lord when he cometh shall find so doing. Verily I say unto you, That he shall make him ruler over all his goods. But and if that evil servant shall say in his heart, My lord delayeth his coming; And shall begin to smite his fellowservants, and to eat and drink with the drunken; The lord of that servant shall come in a day when he looketh not for him, and in an hour that he is not aware of, And shall cut him asunder, and appoint him his portion with the hypocrites: there shall be weeping and gnashing of teeth.*

These verses show that the Jewish believer is expected to maintain his own experience in these times, and the Lord's words indicate how He will assess faith when He comes. It is in their works towards their brothers, fellow Jews, some of whom may be facing an extreme predicament. There will still be rich and poor in these times, and for the wealthy there are always more options than for the poor. This is where their love towards the Lord will be demonstrated, for the Jewish experience is one of 'servants' where their works matter, not that of 'sons', the Church, where belief is the only condition of acceptance.

Matthew 25:1-13: *Then shall the kingdom of heaven be likened unto ten virgins, which took their lamps, and went forth to meet the bridegroom. And five of them were wise, and five were foolish. They that were foolish took their lamps, and took no oil with them: But the wise took oil in their vessels with their lamps. While the bridegroom tarried, they all slumbered and slept. And at midnight there was a cry made, Behold, the bridegroom cometh; go ye out to meet him. Then all those virgins arose, and trimmed their lamps. And the foolish said unto the wise, Give us of your oil; for our lamps are gone out. But the wise answered, saying, Not so; lest there be not enough for us and you: but go ye rather to them that sell, and buy for yourselves. And while they went to buy, the bridegroom came; and they that were ready went in with him to the marriage: and the door was shut. Afterward came also the other virgins, saying, Lord, Lord, open to us. But He answered and said, Verily I say unto you, I know you not. Watch therefore, for ye know neither the day nor the hour wherein the Son of Man cometh.*

The difference between the foolish and wise in this case is demonstrated in the foresight and general attitude towards the event which the wise exhibit. Recognising that they do not know how long they will be expected to wait, they prepare themselves for every eventuality. They are also wise in that they do not give away the oil they have prepared, or become distracted by others to the extent that they lose out themselves. This does not reflect on their generosity, but rather on their determination to get into the celebrations. The Lord goes to great lengths to stress that it is the responsibility of each Jew, as His servant, to fulfil his obligation to be faithful to the end. There are no exceptions, and when the door is closed the celebrations will begin, but those who are not ready will not get in.

Matthew 25:14-30: *For the kingdom of heaven is as a man travelling into a far country, who called his own servants, and delivered unto them his goods. And unto one he gave five talents, to another two, and to another one; to every man according to his several ability; and straightway took his journey. Then he that had received the five talents went and traded with the same, and made them other five talents. And likewise he that had received two, he also gained other two. But he that had received one went and digged in the earth, and hid his lord's money. After a long time the lord of those servants cometh, and reckoneth with them. And so he that had received five talents came and brought other five talents, saying, Lord, thou deliveredst unto me five talents: behold, I have gained beside them five talents more. His lord said unto him, Well done, thou good and faithful servant: thou hast been faithful over a few things, I will make thee ruler over many things: enter thou into the joy of thy lord. He also that had received two talents came and said, Lord, thou deliveredst unto me two talents: behold, I have gained two other talents beside them. His lord said unto him, Well done, good and faithful servant; thou hast been faithful over a few things, I will make thee ruler over many things: enter thou into the joy of thy lord. Then he which had received the one talent came and said, Lord, I knew thee that thou art an hard man, reaping where thou hast not sown, and gathering where thou hast not strawed: And I was afraid, and went and hid thy talent in the earth: lo, there thou hast that is thine. His lord answered and said unto him, Thou wicked and slothful servant, thou knewest that I reap where I sowed not, and gather where I have not strawed: Thou oughtest therefore to have put my money to the exchangers, and then at my coming I should have received mine own with usury. Take therefore the talent from him, and give it unto him which hath ten talents. For unto every one that hath shall be given, and he shall have abundance: but from him that hath not shall be taken away even that which he hath. And cast ye the unprofitable servant into outer darkness: there shall be weeping and gnashing of teeth.*

Again the emphasis is on service, duty and faithfulness. The example given here shows that the diligent will increase what they have, but there is enough time given so that each can prove his worth. Those that waste the opportunity will have had plenty of time to reconsider and change, and when the Lord returns, there are no excuses. It is the condition of the servant at the Lord's return that determines his future, whether he is rewarded or judged.

Matthew 25:31-46: *When the Son of Man shall come in His glory, and all the holy angels with Him, then shall He sit upon the throne of His glory: And before Him shall be gathered all nations: and He shall separate them one from another, as a shepherd divideth his sheep from the goats: And He shall set the sheep on His right hand, but the goats on the left. Then shall the King say unto them on His right hand, Come, ye blessed of My Father, inherit the kingdom prepared for you from the foundation of the world: For I was an hungred, and ye gave Me meat: I was thirsty, and ye gave Me drink: I was a stranger, and ye took Me in: Naked, and ye clothed Me: I was sick, and ye visited Me: I was in prison, and ye came unto Me. Then shall the righteous answer Him, saying, Lord, when saw we Thee an hungred, and fed Thee? or thirsty, and gave Thee drink? When saw we Thee a stranger, and took Thee in? or naked, and clothed Thee? Or when saw we Thee sick, or in prison, and came unto Thee? And the King shall answer and say unto them, Verily I say unto you, Inasmuch as ye have done it unto one of the least of these My brethren, ye have done it unto Me. Then shall He say also unto them on the left hand, Depart from Me, ye cursed, into everlasting fire, prepared for the devil and his angels: For I was an hungred, and ye gave Me no meat: I was thirsty, and ye gave me no drink: I was a stranger, and ye took Me not in: naked, and ye clothed Me not: sick, and in prison, and ye visited Me not. Then shall they also answer Him, saying, Lord, when saw we Thee an hungred, or athirst, or a stranger, or naked, or sick, or in prison, and did not minister unto Thee? Then shall He answer them, saying, Verily I say unto you, Inasmuch as ye did it not to one of the least of these, ye did it not to Me. And these shall go away into everlasting punishment: but the righteous into life eternal.*

Again a wonderful simplicity in the revealing of what the Lord expects at His coming. It is not about outward show but rather the heart of His servant towards his fellow when he feels he is not being watched or judged. The Lord shows what he expects in its simplest form. Hence the surprise of the righteous, and the equal surprise of the wicked, when standing before the Lord to give account. These conditions will also apply in the judgment of the nations at the end, for those nations that have shown pity on Israel in their desperate times can surely expect favour from the Lord Himself, in His future reign.

Mark's account:

Mark 13:1-13: *And as He went out of the temple, one of His disciples saith unto Him, Master, see what manner of stones and what buildings are here! And Jesus answering said unto him, Seest thou these great buildings? there shall not be left one stone upon another, that shall not be thrown down. And as He sat upon the mount of Olives over against the temple, Peter and James and John and Andrew asked Him privately, Tell us, when shall these things be? and what shall be the sign when all these things shall be fulfilled? And Jesus answering them began to say, Take heed lest any man deceive you: For many shall come in My name, saying, I am Christ; and shall deceive many. And when ye shall hear of wars and rumours of wars, be ye not troubled: for such things must needs be; but the end shall not be yet. For nation shall rise against nation, and kingdom against kingdom: and there shall be earthquakes in divers places, and there shall be famines and troubles: these are the beginnings of sorrows. But take heed to yourselves: for they shall deliver you up to councils; and in the synagogues ye shall be beaten: and ye shall be brought before rulers and kings for My sake, for a testimony against them. And the gospel must first be published among all nations. But when they shall lead you, and deliver you up, take no thought beforehand what ye shall speak, neither do ye premeditate: but whatsoever shall be given you in that hour, that speak ye: for it is not ye that speak, but the Holy Ghost. Now the brother shall betray the brother to death, and the father the son; and children shall rise up against their parents, and shall cause them to be put to death. And ye shall be hated of all men for My name's sake: but he that shall endure unto the end, the same shall be saved.*

A similar warning about false prophets, but here we also see that in the first half of the week, there will be a lot of internal persecution and opposition to those who follow the preaching of the Kingdom. Their witness at such hearings within the synagogues is from the Holy Spirit Himself. This does not guarantee their safety however, for many are killed at this time, even before the real persecution starts from the middle of the week.

Mark 13:14-23: *But when ye shall see the abomination of desolation, spoken of by Daniel the prophet, standing where it ought not, (let him that readeth understand,) then let them that be in Judaea flee to the mountains: And let him that is on the housetop not go down into the house, neither enter therein, to take any thing out of his house: And let him that is in the field not turn back again for to take up his garment. But woe to them that are with child, and to them that give suck in those days! And pray ye that your flight be not in the winter. For in those days shall be affliction, such as was not from the beginning of the creation which God created unto this time, neither shall be. And except that the Lord had shortened those days, no flesh should be saved: but for the elect's sake, whom He hath chosen, He hath shortened the days. And then if any man shall say to you, Lo, here is Christ; or, lo, He is there; believe him not: For false Christs and false prophets shall rise, and shall shew signs and wonders, to seduce, if it were possible, even the elect. But take ye heed: behold, I have foretold you all things.*

Again, the abomination of desolation divides the period, and is the signal for real flight from Judaea and Jerusalem. The sense of urgency here is real, for all those caught will face interrogation, in order to seduce them from their belief. There is no deliverance at this time, except to escape, and the worst enemy seems to be the 'False Christs and Prophets', whose methods are lethal.

Mark 13:24-27: *But in those days, after that tribulation, the sun shall be darkened, and the moon shall not give her light, and the stars of heaven shall fall, and the powers that are in heaven shall be shaken. And then shall they see the Son of Man coming in the clouds with great power and glory. And then shall He send His angels, and shall gather together His elect from the four winds, from the uttermost part of the earth to the uttermost part of heaven.*

Here the Lord speaks about an indeterminate period after the events of the 'great tribulation' where the signs given are in the heavens, and the Jews will return to Israel, from wherever they have escaped.

Mark 13:28-37: *Now learn a parable of the fig tree; When her branch is yet tender, and putteth forth leaves, ye know that summer is near: So ye in like manner, when ye shall see these things come to pass, know that it is nigh, even at the doors. Verily I say unto you, that this generation shall not pass, till all these things be done. Heaven and earth shall pass away: but My words shall not pass away. But of that day and that hour knoweth no man, no, not the angels which are in heaven, neither the Son, but the Father. Take ye heed, watch and pray: for ye know not when the time is. For the Son of Man is as a man taking a far journey, who left his house, and gave authority to his servants, and to every man his work, and commanded the porter to watch. Watch ye therefore: for ye know not when the master of the house cometh, at even, or at midnight, or at the cockcrowing, or in the morning: Lest coming suddenly He find you sleeping. And what I say unto you I say unto all, Watch.*

The emphasis again is on watchfulness, and the fact that no one knows the exact time of the Lord's return, so there will be no time to put things right, if they are not already right. The servant has to be faithful at all times, to avoid being caught out at the Lord's coming.

Luke's first account

Luke 17:20-21: *And when He was demanded of the Pharisees, when the kingdom of God should come, He answered them and said, The kingdom of God cometh not with observation: Neither shall they say, Lo here! or, lo there! for, behold, the kingdom of God is within you.*

The Lord's response to the Pharisees demand for revelation is far shorter, for He did not recognize their authority in the slightest. To them, He says that nothing is going to be revealed by their 'observations' (the Greek word used is *parateresis* always used in a bad sense, as in waiting for opportunity to find fault), they will not be given any revelation because they could not recognise the Lord, even when He was standing among them. They and their like will not see the signs, because they will not ask Him for their eyes to be opened.

Luke 17:22-37: *And He said unto the disciples, The days will come, when ye shall desire to see one of the days of the Son of Man, and ye shall not see it. And they shall say to you, See here; or, see there: go not after them, nor follow them. For as the lightning, that lighteneth out of the one part under heaven, shineth unto the other part under heaven; so shall also the Son of Man be in His day. But first must He suffer many things, and be rejected of this generation. And as it was in the days of Noe, so shall it be also in the days of the Son of Man. They did eat, they drank, they married wives, they were given in marriage, until the day that Noe entered into the ark, and the flood came, and destroyed them all. Likewise also as it was in the days of Lot; they did eat, they drank, they bought, they sold, they planted, they builded; But the same day that Lot went out of Sodom it rained fire and brimstone from heaven, and destroyed them all. Even thus shall it be in the day when the Son of Man is revealed. In that day, he which shall be upon the housetop, and his stuff in the house, let him not come down to take it away: and he that is in the field, let him likewise not return back. Remember Lot's wife. Whosoever shall seek to save his life shall lose it; and whosoever shall lose his life shall preserve it. I tell you, in that night there shall be two men in one bed; the one shall be taken, and the other shall be left. Two women shall be grinding together; the one shall be taken, and the other left. Two men shall be in the field; the one shall be taken, and the other left. And they answered and said unto Him, Where, Lord? And He said unto them, Wheresoever the body is, thither will the eagles be gathered together.*

The Lord's enigmatic reply to the disciple's question as to where the people who are taken go has been the subject of much conjecture. A simple explanation is that the eagles go to where the food is, and they know at the time where to go, because their senses are attuned to their environment. Those who are ready will know where to go at the time, but the Lord is not going to reveal this place to anyone beforehand.

Luke's second account

Luke 21:5-24: *And as some spake of the temple, how it was adorned with goodly stones and gifts, He said, As for these things which ye behold, the days will come, in the which there shall not be left one stone upon another, that shall not be thrown down. And they asked Him, saying, Master, but when shall these things be? and what sign will there be when these things shall come to pass? And He said , Take heed that ye be not deceived: for many shall come in My name, saying, I am Christ; and the time draweth near: go ye not therefore after them. But when ye shall hear of wars and commotions, be not terrified: for these things must first come to pass; but the end is not by and by. Then said He unto them, Nation shall rise against nation, and kingdom against kingdom: And great earthquakes shall be in divers places, and famines, and pestilences; and fearful sights and great signs shall there be from heaven. But before all these, they shall lay their hands on you, and persecute you, delivering you up to the synagogues, and into prisons, being brought before kings and rulers for My name's sake. And it shall turn to you for a testimony. Settle it therefore in your hearts, not to meditate before what ye shall answer: For I will give you a mouth and wisdom, which all your adversaries shall not be able to gainsay nor resist. And ye shall be betrayed both by parents, and brethren, and kinsfolks, and friends; and some of you shall they cause to be put to death. And ye shall be hated of all men for My name's sake. But there shall not an hair of your head perish. In your patience possess ye your souls. And when ye shall see Jerusalem compassed with armies, then know that the desolation thereof is nigh. Then let them which are in Judaea flee to the mountains; and let them which are in the midst of it depart out; and let not them that are in the countries enter thereinto. For these be the days of vengeance, that all things which are written may be fulfilled. But woe unto them that are with child, and to them that give suck, in those days! for there shall be great distress in the land, and wrath upon this people. And they shall fall by the edge of the sword, and shall be led away captive into all nations: and Jerusalem shall be trodden down of the Gentiles, until the times of the Gentiles be fulfilled.*

A further indication of the time to flee is 'when ye shall see Jerusalem compassed with armies then know that the desolation thereof is nigh'. Again the advice is to go to the mountains, and to avoid the city itself. This suggests that the escape route through the mountains must be the only place free from waiting armies, which again implies the Lord's intervention, in the division of the Mount of Olives. This also shows that the Beast takes Jerusalem and establishes the 'abomination that makes desolate' by force, and although his rise to power is by statesmanship, his final weapon is military force, and with the aim of the destruction of God's people.

Luke 21:25-31: *And there shall be signs in the sun, and in the moon, and in the stars; and upon the earth distress of nations, with perplexity; the sea and the waves roaring; Men's hearts failing them for fear, and for looking after those things which are coming on the earth: for the powers of heaven shall be shaken. And then shall they see the Son of Man coming in a cloud with power and great glory. And when these things begin to come to pass, then look up, and lift up your heads; for your redemption draweth nigh. And He spake to them a parable; Behold the fig tree, and all the trees; When they now shoot forth, ye see and know of your own selves that summer is now nigh at hand. So likewise ye, when ye see these things come to pass, know ye that the kingdom of God is nigh at hand.*

This would suggest that a rise in Israelite nationalism, the 'fig tree', the stirrings of the nation towards the Lord, nationalism amongst other nations, for example surrounding independent nations, is a feature to look for in these times. It is undeniable that in several countries, Russia and Africa being two good examples, there have been ethnic divisions into fiercely independent states, and that many of these changes have been driven by Muslim extremism.

Luke 21:32-38: *Verily I say unto you, This generation shall not pass away, till all be fulfilled. Heaven and earth shall pass away: but My words shall not pass away. And take heed to yourselves, lest at any time your hearts be overcharged with surfeiting, and drunkenness, and cares of this life, and so that day come upon you unawares. For as a snare shall it come on all them that dwell on the face of the whole earth. Watch ye therefore, and pray always, that ye may be accounted worthy to escape all these things that shall come to pass, and to stand before the Son of Man. And in the day time He was teaching in the temple; and at night He went out, and abode in the mount that is called the mount of Olives.*

And all the people came early in the morning to Him in the temple, for to hear Him.

The warnings are loud and clear from the Lord's words to His nation Israel that the end times are only going to be visible for those who are looking for their Lord. The Jewish mockers of scripture and prophecy, who are 'doing fine without the Lord, thank you very much', are in danger of being caught unawares when the time comes, and of leaving it too late.

The Lord expects to find faithfulness in His people, and the reintroduction of the preaching of the Kingdom heralds the destruction of Jerusalem and the persecution of the Jewish people. The prudent in these times should get out, but this will be easier for some than for others. Those left at the end will be given an escape route, but they need to be alert to the scriptures and the signs of the times, or they will miss the opportunity to go. The faithful are then expected to wait till these things are played out, and then will come their deliverance. The most dangerous influence will be the false messiahs, prophets, and teachers who will spring up in these times.

Perhaps it is for this reason that the Lord gave His answers in the simplest of terms, in order to give a straightforward template for the Jews in their hour of need, which is yet to come. There will also be ministry for them from men raised up at the time, including the two witnesses of Revelation. The Jews are not expected to look for their deliverer, for He will appear in the most undeniable form, when He does come for them.

CHAPTER FIVE

PETER AND PROPHECY

Although Peter was never given the same level of understanding of the end times that John and Paul enjoyed, nevertheless he, along with the other apostles, was given a privileged insight into what this involved for his own people during his time with the Lord. It is this understanding that he passes on to the strangers scattered (the Diaspora, or Christian Jews) outside Israel. Peter is not attempting in his letters to explain the mysteries of the Church, as his later [26]ministry was confined to the Jews anyway. It is quite possible that he struggled with these things himself, but in no way does he seek to undermine Paul's writings, which he must have [27]been fully aware of.

Peter has a valid witness of his own, but similar to the Lord's in speaking to the Jews of the end times. It is evident that Peter is still looking forward to the Lord's coming, for this doctrine underpins both of his epistles, and the text shows that he still hoped that the Lord's coming was near for His people. The mystery of the Church was news to Peter as well as others, and these words, given in a simple style not unlike the Lord's own words, should serve as an encouragement for the latter-day Jew, whose hope is of the Lord's coming, both to deliver him from persecution, and to set up His everlasting kingdom.

26. Galatians 2:7
27. The accepted date for Peter's first letter is 60AD, and of Paul's first epistle to Thessalonica, 52AD.

1 Peter 1:1-13: *Peter, an apostle of Jesus Christ, to the strangers scattered throughout Pontus, Galatia, Cappadocia, Asia, and Bithynia, Elect according to the foreknowledge of God the Father, through sanctification of the Spirit, unto obedience and sprinkling of the blood of Jesus Christ: Grace unto you, and peace, be multiplied. Blessed be the God and Father of our Lord Jesus Christ, which according to His abundant mercy hath begotten us again unto a lively hope by the resurrection of Jesus Christ from the dead, To an inheritance incorruptible, and undefiled, and that fadeth not away, reserved in heaven for you, Who are kept by the power of God through faith unto salvation ready to be revealed in the last time. Wherein ye greatly rejoice, though now for a season, if need be, ye are in heaviness through manifold temptations: That the trial of your faith, being much more precious than of gold that perisheth, though it be tried with fire, might be found unto praise and honour and glory at the appearing of Jesus Christ: Whom having not seen, ye love; in Whom, though now ye see Him not, yet believing, ye rejoice with joy unspeakable and full of glory: Receiving the end of your faith, even the salvation of your souls. Of which salvation the prophets have enquired and searched diligently, who prophesied of the grace that should come unto you: Searching what, or what manner of time the Spirit of Christ which was in them did signify, when it testified beforehand the sufferings of Christ, and the glory that should follow. Unto whom it was revealed, that not unto themselves, but unto us they did minister the things, which are now reported unto you by them that have preached the gospel unto you with the Holy Ghost sent down from heaven; which things the angels desire to look into. Wherefore gird up the loins of your mind, be sober, and hope to the end for the grace that is to be brought unto you at the revelation of Jesus Christ;*

1 Peter 4:7-19: *But the end of all things is at hand: be ye therefore sober, and watch unto prayer. And above all things have fervent charity*

among yourselves: for charity shall cover the multitude of sins. Use hospitality one to another without grudging. As every man hath received the gift, even so minister the same one to another, as good stewards of the manifold grace of God. If any man speak, let him speak as the oracles of God; if any man minister, let him do it as of the ability which God giveth: that God in all things may be glorified through Jesus Christ, to Whom be praise and dominion for ever and ever. Amen. Beloved, think it not strange concerning the fiery trial which is to try you, as though some strange thing happened unto you: But rejoice, inasmuch as ye are partakers of Christ's sufferings; that, when His glory shall be revealed, ye may be glad also with exceeding joy. If ye be reproached for the name of Christ, happy are ye; for the spirit of glory and of God resteth upon you: on their part He is evil spoken of, but on your part He is glorified. But let none of you suffer as a murderer, or as a thief, or as an evildoer, or as a busybody in other men's matters. Yet if any man suffer as a Christian, let him not be ashamed; but let him glorify God on this behalf. For the time is come that judgment must begin at the house of God: and if it first begin at us, what shall the end be of them that obey not the gospel of God? And if the righteous scarcely be saved, where shall the ungodly and the sinner appear? Wherefore let them that suffer according to the will of God commit the keeping of their souls to Him in well doing, as unto a faithful Creator.

Peter's concern is for the practical nature of the believer's walk, that is, how they should behave towards one another. The emphasis is on the main commandment of the Lord that they should love one another in a practical sense in their day-to-day dealings, and that their ministry together is to the glory of God, rather than self.

He also wants to give some perspective on their sufferings, which will surely come on all those who are seeking God's will, in an alien society. Notwithstanding this, he encourages them not to bring these sufferings on themselves needlessly, by acting stupidly and provoking a reaction from others. He again refers to the fact that the Lord is coming as a judge, as well as a redeemer, so they should wait patiently in their troubles for the Lord to come and put things right. Judgement of course, when it comes, will begin at the house of God, in the very heavens themselves, when Satan will be [28]cast out of God's presence, and will then stir up the world to try and bring it into the same condemnation that he faces.

1 Peter 5:1-4: *The elders which are among you I exhort, who am also an elder, and a witness of the sufferings of Christ, and also a partaker of the glory that shall be revealed: Feed the flock of God which is among you, taking the oversight thereof, not by constraint, but willingly; not for filthy lucre, but of a ready mind; Neither as being lords over God's heritage, but being ensamples to the flock. And when the Chief Shepherd shall appear, ye shall receive a crown of glory that fadeth not away.*

Peter's message to the church elders, those with a responsibility for the flock, is that their reward is the crown of glory that they will be given at the Lord's appearing. This reward is for those who have ministered with a 'ready mind' and who realise that there is no fleshly reward for their labours, and have therefore done it in the right spirit. For these the reward does not tarnish over time, they have chosen the better part, and are noted eternally for their faithfulness.

1 Peter 5:5-8: *Likewise, ye younger, submit yourselves unto the elder. Yea, all of you be subject one to another, and be clothed with humility:*

28. Revelation 12:9-12.

for God resisteth the proud, and giveth grace to the humble. Humble
yourselves therefore under the mighty hand of God, that He may exalt
you in due time: Casting all your care upon Him; for He careth for you.
Be sober, be vigilant; because your adversary the devil, as a roaring lion,
walketh about, seeking whom he may devour:

Again, a consistent message for the end times is sobriety and
vigilance, as the latter is not possible without the former. To the
drunkard, events come upon him unawares, when his guard is
down. The many references to remaining sober must reflect
those pressures on us in these last days to succumb to
drunkenness and excess. Whilst few would want to return to the
enforced religiousness of puritan times, there is a lamentable
tendency for believers, or those claiming a form of belief, to
conform to the normally accepted standards of their worldly
contemporaries, such as excessive drinking. It is far better to
accept the separation, which is the holiness we have been called
to. Although the Christian believer is not under any law, and has
perfect liberty, he also has the liberty to choose to be separate
from this world, which is altogether his best option.

Our [29]salvation does not depend on whether we are alert to
signs of the Lord's coming, or not, but rather on our belief on
Him as the Son of God, Who raised Him again from the dead.
Nevertheless, we are expected to be aware of the times in which
we live, and not subscribe willingly to the weakness of the flesh.
Peter confirms that the true believer is constantly looking
towards his own redemption. He stands in the true grace of God.

1 Peter 5:9-14: *Whom resist stedfast in the faith, knowing that the*
same afflictions are accomplished in your brethren that are in the world.

29. 1 Thessalonians 4:14.

But the God of all grace, Who hath called us unto His eternal glory by Christ Jesus, after that ye have suffered a while, make you perfect, stablish, strengthen, settle you. To Him be glory and dominion for ever and ever. Amen. By Silvanus, a faithful brother unto you, as I suppose, I have written briefly, exhorting, and testifying that this is the true grace of God wherein ye stand. The church that is at Babylon, elected together with you, saluteth you; and so doth Marcus my son. Greet ye one another with a kiss of charity. Peace be with you all that are in Christ Jesus. Amen.

2 Peter 1:1-11: *Simon Peter, a servant and an apostle of Jesus Christ, to them that have obtained like precious faith with us through the righteousness of God and our Saviour Jesus Christ: Grace and peace be multiplied unto you through the knowledge of God, and of Jesus our Lord, According as His divine power hath given unto us all things that pertain unto life and godliness, through the knowledge of Him that hath called us to glory and virtue: Whereby are given unto us exceeding great and precious promises: that by these ye might be partakers of the divine nature, having escaped the corruption that is in the world through lust. And beside this, giving all diligence, add to your faith virtue; and to virtue knowledge; And to knowledge temperance; and to temperance patience; and to patience godliness; And to godliness brotherly kindness; and to brotherly kindness charity. For if these things be in you, and abound, they make you that ye shall neither be barren nor unfruitful in the knowledge of our Lord Jesus Christ. But he that lacketh these things is blind, and cannot see afar off, and hath forgotten that he was purged from his old sins. Wherefore the rather, brethren, give diligence to make your calling and election sure: for if ye do these things, ye shall never fall: For so an entrance shall be ministered unto you abundantly into the everlasting kingdom of our Lord and Saviour Jesus Christ.*

Peter continues in his second epistle to establish these Jewish believers, and his advice is to build on their faith, the basis of their salvation, in furthering their experience with God. The end of this is charity, or grace, but notice how he develops this:

Giving all diligence, ie speedily, or make it your business, to add:

Virtue, or **manliness**, in the sense of excelling, then **knowledge**, then **temperance,** or **self-control**, which will ensure that our knowledge does not 'puff us up'. To this add **patience**, which is cheerfulness or optimism, then **godliness,** which is piety in the sense of taking things seriously, not flippantly. Then to add **brotherly kindness**, which is the *agape* love of the early church, love for one another, and finally **charity**, which is love in a broader sense that extends to all.

Peter's view is that all these things working in us, and abounding, make us stable or grounded believers. Those who neglect these things put themselves in a dangerous position, weakened through their forgetfulness of just Who had died for them.

2 Peter 1:12-21: *Wherefore I will not be negligent to put you always in remembrance of these things, though ye know them, and be established in the present truth. Yea, I think it meet, as long as I am in this tabernacle, to stir you up by putting you in remembrance; Knowing that shortly I must put off this my tabernacle, even as our Lord Jesus Christ hath shewed me. Moreover I will endeavour that ye may be able after my decease to have these things always in remembrance. For we have not followed cunningly devised fables, when we made known unto you the power and coming of our Lord Jesus Christ, but were eyewitnesses of His majesty. For He received from God the Father honour and glory, when there came such a voice to Him from the excellent glory, This is*

My beloved Son, in Whom I am well pleased. And this voice which came from heaven we heard, when we were with Him in the holy mount. We have also a more sure Word of prophecy; whereunto ye do well that ye take heed, as unto a light that shineth in a dark place, until the day dawn, and the day star arise in your hearts: Knowing this first, that no prophecy of the scripture is of any private interpretation. For the prophecy came not in old time by the will of man: but holy men of God spake as they were moved by the Holy Ghost.

Interestingly, whilst Peter considers himself an eyewitness, his appeal to them is the 'more sure Word of prophecy' the scriptures, which he puts above his own ministry and witness, and commends these believers for their adherence to the Word.

2 Peter 2:1-22: *But there were false prophets also among the people, even as there shall be false teachers among you, who privily shall bring in damnable heresies, even denying the Lord that bought them, and bring upon themselves swift destruction. And many shall follow their pernicious ways; by reason of whom the way of truth shall be evil spoken of. And through covetousness shall they with feigned words make merchandise of you: whose judgment now of a long time lingereth not, and their damnation slumbereth not. For if God spared not the angels that sinned, but cast them down to hell, and delivered them into chains of darkness, to be reserved unto judgment; And spared not the old world, but saved Noah the eighth person, a preacher of righteousness, bringing in the flood upon the world of the ungodly; And turning the cities of Sodom and Gomorrha into ashes condemned them with an overthrow, making them an ensample unto those that after should live ungodly. And delivered just Lot, vexed with the filthy conversation of the wicked: (For that righteous man dwelling among them, in seeing and hearing, vexed his righteous soul from day to day with their unlawful deeds;)*

The Lord knoweth how to deliver the godly out of temptations, and to reserve the unjust unto the day of judgment to be punished. But chiefly them that walk after the flesh in the lust of uncleanness, and despise government. Presumptuous are they, selfwilled, they are not afraid to speak evil of dignities. Whereas angels, which are greater in power and might, bring not railing accusation against them before the Lord. But these, as natural brute beasts, made to be taken and destroyed, speak evil of the things that they understand not; and shall utterly perish in their own corruption; And shall receive the reward of unrighteousness, as they that count it pleasure to riot in the day time. Spots they are and blemishes, sporting themselves with their own deceivings while they feast with you; Having eyes full of adultery, and that cannot cease from sin; beguiling unstable souls: an heart they have exercised with covetous practices; cursed children: Which have forsaken the right way, and are gone astray, following the way of Balaam the son of Bosor, who loved the wages of unrighteousness; But was rebuked for his iniquity: the dumb ass speaking with man's voice forbad the madness of the prophet. These are wells without water, clouds that are carried with a tempest; to whom the mist of darkness is reserved for ever. For when they speak great swelling words of vanity, they allure through the lusts of the flesh, through much wantonness, those that were clean escaped from them who live in error. While they promise them liberty, they themselves are the servants of corruption: for of whom a man is overcome, of the same is he brought in bondage. For if after they have escaped the pollutions of the world through the knowledge of the Lord and Saviour Jesus Christ, they are again entangled therein, and overcome, the latter end is worse with them than the beginning. For it had been better for them not to have known the way of righteousness, than, after they have known it, to turn from the holy commandment delivered unto them. But it is happened unto them according to the true proverb, The dog is turned to his own vomit again; and the sow that was washed to her wallowing in the mire.

Peter echoes the Lord's teachings here, as an eyewitness of them, that within the churches there will be those teaching different doctrines. Namely, versions of the truth which they imagine from out of their own hearts, whether being loosely based on the law, the scriptures or fables, but with the purpose of gaining mastery over sections of the people for their own ends. Make no mistake, they will convince many, but also turn away many from the truth who might otherwise have been persuaded of salvation, but who, having seen the hypocrisy and the excesses of these teachers and their followers, turn away from it.

As the time draws nearer, so this form of apostasy will become more apparent, and the false teachers will appear, often looking better than the real thing. If it were not for the Lord protecting His own, then it is unlikely that any would survive at all. Certainly for the Jews in the last times, their need is to thoroughly know their place in the Lord's plan, and in particular to be aware of what the scriptures say, in order to spot the counterfeit teaching that will be widespread. Peter warns against the *many* false teachers, as the Lord did, for it is not only the 'Beast' that is a danger, but also those within the assemblies, who have other motives rather than the care of the churches. This of course is the job of the pastor, who is compared to the shepherd, who sits in the gate watching out for any predators. The first line of defence is to know the doctrines that apply to us, and are relevant to our own dispensation, or time.

One way false doctrines may be introduced is by the denial of the teachings about the end days, the 'scoffers' or deriders, who undermine prophecy by pointing to the fact that the prophesied judgement has not happened yet, and therefore is not going to. The man with the board claiming that 'the end of the world is nigh' is ridiculed as an example of religious stupidity, although in fact he is right. But these people are sophisticated in their knowledge and reasoning, and appeal to the modern day philosophies of reason and enlightened argument, again conforming to the sensible majority. We, however, walk by faith, and do not have to justify our belief to anyone. It is simple for us, as we are only required to believe what is written, after having rightly divided the truth.

2 Peter 3:1-7: *This second epistle, beloved, I now write unto you; in both which I stir up your pure minds by way of remembrance: That ye may be mindful of the words which were spoken before by the holy prophets, and of the commandment of us the apostles of the Lord and Saviour: Knowing this first, that there shall come in the last days scoffers, walking after their own lusts, And saying, Where is the promise of His coming? for since the fathers fell asleep, all things continue as they were from the beginning of the creation. For this they willingly are ignorant of, that by the Word of God the heavens were of old, and the earth standing out of the water and in the water: Whereby the world that then was, being overflowed with water, perished: But the heavens and the earth, which are now, by the same Word are kept in store, reserved unto fire against the day of judgment and perdition of ungodly men.*

Peter knows however that these scoffers simply do not recognise the greatness of the Lord, Who will not react to such provocation to prove Himself, until He is ready to. They mistake His restraint for weakness, but fail to recognise that their judgement when it comes, will be the more severe because of the grace initially shown to them.

2 Peter 3:8-10: *But, beloved, be not ignorant of this one thing, that one day is with the Lord as a thousand years, and a thousand years as*

one day. The Lord is not slack concerning His promise, as some men count slackness; but is longsuffering to us-ward, not willing that any should perish, but that all should come to repentance. But the day of the Lord will come as a thief in the night; in the which the heavens shall pass away with a great noise, and the elements shall melt with fervent heat, the earth also and the works that are therein shall be burned up.

Peter here of course refers to the Day of the Lord, which is the Jewish part of the Lord's coming. He does not refer to doctrines for the church of the Gentiles, which is an area that he knows is best left to Paul to explain. The thief in the night is a danger to the unaware, the drunk, and the sleeping, who are all unprepared. To these who have not availed themselves of the time they have been extended, the Lord's coming will be a disaster, and on them will come the persecution, particularly in Jerusalem, but also in other places. We have to be careful here to distinguish between the Lord's coming for His people to set them as rulers over the earth, and the final onslaught after the [30]millennium, or thousand-year reign, after which there is a new heaven and a new earth. His question therefore to them is, in the light of this, what manner of persons ought they to be, if they are to partake of God's eventual plan for them?

2 Peter 3:11-18: *Seeing then that all these things shall be dissolved, what manner of persons ought ye to be in all holy conversation and godliness, Looking for and hasting unto the coming of the day of God, wherein the heavens being on fire shall be dissolved, and the elements shall melt with fervent heat? Nevertheless we, according to His promise, look for new heavens and a new earth, wherein dwelleth righteousness. Wherefore, beloved, seeing that ye look for such things, be diligent that*

30. This will be discussed further when considering John's writings in Revelation. Paul and Prophecy

ye may be found of Him in peace, without spot, and blameless. And account that the longsuffering of our Lord is salvation; even as our beloved brother Paul also according to the wisdom given unto him hath written unto you; As also in all his epistles, speaking in them of these things; in which are some things hard to be understood, which they that are unlearned and unstable wrest, as they do also the other scriptures, unto their own destruction. Ye therefore, beloved, seeing ye know these things before, beware lest ye also, being led away with the error of the wicked, fall from your own stedfastness. But grow in grace, and in the knowledge of our Lord and Saviour Jesus Christ. To Him be glory both now and for ever. Amen."

To conclude, Peter makes no attempt in his epistles to explain the end days in the same way that the Lord, and John and Paul did. His letters are more an exhortation to these believers to hold fast to what they have, and for them to bear in mind the fact that the Lord will come, and when He does He will expect to find them waiting in His commandments, basically in love towards one another.

These verses should also be of help to the latter-day Jew who finds himself caught up in the events of the 'Day of the Lord'. Evidently from Peter's writings, this is not simply a day, but the time from which judgement commences, both in the heavens and on the earth. He very much defers to the teachings of Paul, and sees himself as one who has witnessed the truth of the Lord, and whose job it is to feed the flock. Whatever mistakes Peter made in his early days, often putting his foot in it as the spokesman for the others, he remained faithful to His Lord, even to death.

CHAPTER SIX

PAUL AND PROPHECY

For those of us in the Church, Paul, who was the apostle to the Gentiles, is the person who will shed most light on what the expectation of the Christian should be in these last days. He wrote and spoke often about the end times, being an authority on both the Jewish promises and those to the Church, the body of our Lord. Mainly he expounds on the subject in his two letters to the Thessalonians, but in most of his writings we can find references to the Lord's coming, either for the Church or for the nation Israel. We will consider his writings in the order they are given in scripture, and draw our conclusions from them, but first:

Acts 1:6-11: *When they therefore were come together, they asked of Him, saying, Lord, wilt Thou at this time restore again the kingdom to Israel? And He said unto them, It is not for you to know the times or the seasons, which the Father hath put in His own power. But ye shall receive power, after that the Holy Ghost is come upon you: and ye shall be witnesses unto Me both in Jerusalem, and in all Judaea, and in Samaria, and unto the uttermost part of the earth. And when He had spoken these things, while they beheld, He was taken up; and a cloud received Him out of their sight. And while they looked stedfastly toward heaven as He went up, behold, two men stood by them in white apparel;*

Which also said, Ye men of Galilee, why stand ye gazing up into heaven? this same Jesus, which is taken up from you into heaven, shall so come in like manner as ye have seen Him go into heaven.

After the Lord's resurrection, the disciples question was not about the Baptism of the Holy Spirit, which was what He wanted to speak to them about, but rather about the restoration of the kingdom, Israel's promised rule on the earth, with which they were more concerned at the time. However, they soon realise after Pentecost that the outpouring of the Spirit was a part of the last days, and Peter, quoting from Joel says:

Acts 2:16-21: *But this is that which was spoken by the prophet Joel; And it shall come to pass in the last days, saith God, I will pour out of My Spirit upon all flesh: and your sons and your daughters shall prophesy, and your young men shall see visions, and your old men shall dream dreams: And on My servants and on My handmaidens I will pour out in those days of My Spirit; and they shall prophesy: And I will shew wonders in heaven above, and signs in the earth beneath; blood, and fire, and vapour of smoke: The sun shall be turned into darkness, and the moon into blood, before that great and notable day of the Lord come: And it shall come to pass, that whosoever shall call on the name of the Lord shall be saved.*

The point here is that Peter and the other disciples consider that these were the last days, and that the sign of speaking in tongues was the manifestation of the outpouring of the Spirit prophesied by Joel. These verses also include the expression the 'Day of the Lord', and show that before this is ended, there will be great and unmistakeable signs in the heavens, heralding the Lord's return for Israel. However, the Lord has already shown them that the timing of His return was a mystery, but they would not have possibly guessed the length of time that would pass before the real fulfilment of this. Neither would they have suspected that in the middle of this period, following the rejection of their own ministry to Israel, there would be another people formed, who were to be partakers of an entirely separate and heavenly experience, that which we call the Church, or His body.

Paul's first appearance in scripture is as the main persecutor of the early Church, and his zeal for his task indirectly causes the gospel of the kingdom to be preached further afield[31] than it might otherwise have been. Not happy that some were escaping, he follows them up to near Damascus, where the Lord appears to him and makes him an offer he cannot refuse. Paul's fame has preceded him, but from here on he belongs to the Lord, and although he does not know it yet, he is set to become the greatest apostle of them all. Peter is still active at this time, but the ministry he was offered initially was to the Gentile nations. As it turned out, he would never overcome his reluctance to accept non-Jews as believers on an equal footing, despite the vision he had been given regarding [32]Cornelius. In Paul, the Lord had found a man who would do his bidding, and with his track record of persecuting believers, he could never really allow himself to question the Lord's right to save whoever He wished to.

Initially, Paul was the companion of Barnabas in travel, both of them being servants of the Church under the direction of the apostles. It becomes apparent in Acts 13 that the Holy Spirit had a distinct work for Barnabas and Saul, and they are despatched to the distant synagogues, initially with John (Mark) as a minister. There is a change however, described in Acts 13:42-44:

31. Acts 8:3-4.
32. Acts 10 and 11.

And when the Jews were gone out of the synagogue, the Gentiles besought that these words might be preached to them the next Sabbath. Now when the congregation was broken up, many of the Jews and religious proselytes followed Paul and Barnabas: who, speaking to them, persuaded them to continue in the grace of God. And the next Sabbath day came almost the whole city together to hear the Word of God.

This causes a reaction from the Jews, which elicited the response from Barnabas and Paul that they would now go to the Gentiles, in accordance with what they had [33]heard from the Lord, that He had set them to be a 'light to the Gentiles'.

Paul starts to talk about the expectation of both Jew and Gentile believers regarding the Lord's coming, in 1 Corinthians 15. The Gospel, or good news, is the means of salvation, for in it is contained the basics tenet of our belief that *"Christ died for our sins according to the scriptures, and that He was buried, and that He rose again the third day"*.

1 Corinthians 15:1-11: *Moreover, brethren, I declare unto you the gospel which I preached unto you, which also ye have received, and wherein ye stand; By which also ye are saved, if ye keep in memory what I preached unto you, unless ye have believed in vain. For I delivered unto you first of all that which I also received, how that Christ died for our sins according to the scriptures; And that He was buried, and that He rose again the third day according to the scriptures: And that He was seen of Cephas, then of the twelve: After that, He was seen of above five hundred brethren at once; of whom the greater part remain unto this present, but some are fallen asleep. After that, He was seen of James;*

---

33. Isaiah 49:6 This is important, as it shows that the beginnings of the Gentile church through Barnabas and Paul came from what they had been given personally from the Word.

then of all the apostles. And last of all He was seen of me also, as of one born out of due time. For I am the least of the apostles, that am not meet to be called an apostle, because I persecuted the Church of God. But by the grace of God I am what I am: and His grace which was bestowed upon me was not in vain; but I laboured more abundantly than they all: yet not I, but the grace of God which was with me. Therefore whether it were I or they, so we preach, and so ye believed.

So knowing and believing that He is the Son of God, that He died for us, and that He was raised again, is all that is necessary in terms of salvation. But this was the very thing that was being contested, even amongst these believers. Paul reasons with them concerning this, for there is no room for argument. If they believed that the dead could not be raised again, then their faith would be worthless, there would be no remission for their sins, and those that had died would be lost.

Paul maintains that if our Christianity only applies while we are in this life, we might just as well enjoy the things of the flesh, and not regard eternity at all. We would indeed be pitiable, if our belief in an eternal life was an empty one.

1 Corinthians 15:12-19: *Now if Christ be preached that He rose from the dead, how say some among you that there is no resurrection of the dead? But if there be no resurrection of the dead, then is Christ not risen: And if Christ be not risen, then is our preaching vain, and your faith is also vain. Yea, and we are found false witnesses of God; because we have testified of God that He raised up Christ: Whom He raised not up, if so be that the dead rise not. For if the dead rise not, then is not Christ raised: And if Christ be not raised, your faith is vain; ye are yet in your sins. Then they also which are fallen asleep in Christ are perished. If in this life only we have hope in Christ, we are of all men most miserable.*

However, Paul reiterates what he has preached, and what the gospel is based on: The Lord has been raised from the dead, becoming the 'firstfruits' (= first offering) of them that slept, the ones who are also to be raised up in Him. He was the first man raised from the dead, and those who believe in Him shall be raised after Him, at His appearing for them, and us.

1 Corinthians 15:20-23: *But now is Christ risen from the dead, and become the firstfruits of them that slept. For since by man came death, by man came also the resurrection of the dead. For as in Adam all die, even so in Christ shall all be made alive. But every man in his own order: Christ the firstfruits; afterward they that are Christ's at His coming.*

After this comes the 'End', and we know from Daniel's writings that there are events to come concerning Israel and the nations surrounding it in the end days. All enemies are then made subject to The Lord, and even death, which is the result of sin, will be subjugated to Him. He finally hands everything back to God, perfected.

1 Corinthians 15:24-34: *Then cometh the end, when He shall have delivered up the kingdom to God, even the Father; when He shall have put down all rule and all authority and power. For He must reign, till He hath put all enemies under His feet. The last enemy that shall be destroyed is death. For He hath put all things under His feet. But when He saith all things are put under Him, it is manifest that He is excepted, which did put all things under Him. And when all things shall be subdued unto Him, then shall the Son also Himself be subject unto Him that put all things under Him, that God may be all in all. Else what shall they do which are baptized for the dead, if the dead rise not at all? why are they then baptized for the dead? And why stand we in*

jeopardy every hour? I protest by your rejoicing which I have in Christ Jesus our Lord, I die daily. If after the manner of men I have fought with beasts at Ephesus, what advantageth it me, if the dead rise not? let us eat and drink; for to morrow we die. Be not deceived: evil communications corrupt good manners. Awake to righteousness, and sin not; for some have not the knowledge of God: I speak this to your shame.

Those among them who are arguing concerning the resurrection are rightly put in their place for their 'evil communications', for they are sawing away at the very branch they are sitting on, the hope of our resurrection in Him. Paul answers the question regarding baptism for the dead in his epistle to [34]Romans (Romans 6:3-11):

Know ye not, that so many of us as were baptized into Jesus Christ were baptized into His death? Therefore we are buried with Him by baptism into death: that like as Christ was raised up from the dead by the glory of the Father, even so we also should walk in newness of life. For if we have been planted together in the likeness of His death, we shall be also in the likeness of His resurrection: Knowing this, that our old man is crucified with Him, that the body of sin might be destroyed, that henceforth we should not serve sin. For he that is dead is freed from sin. Now if we be dead with Christ, we believe that we shall also live with Him: Knowing that Christ being raised from the dead dieth no more; death hath no more dominion over Him. For in that He died, He died unto sin once: but in that He liveth, He liveth unto God. Likewise reckon ye also yourselves to be dead indeed unto sin, but alive unto God through Jesus Christ our Lord.

34. And also in Colossians 1:18 "Who is the beginning, the firstborn from the dead; that in all things he might have the pre-eminence." See also Colossians 2:12 "Buried with Him in baptism."

This is what he means by being baptized for the dead; it is our baptism into Him, the name of the Lord. Although we still have this body of flesh, it is counted crucified with Him, no longer a hindrance, and we can now consider ourselves alive unto Him, despite the fact that our body has not yet changed. We will receive a new body at His coming, and this is what Paul continues to explain:

1 Corinthians 15:35-50: *But some man will say, How are the dead raised up? and with what body do they come? Thou fool, that which thou sowest is not quickened, except it die: And that which thou sowest, thou sowest not that body that shall be, but bare grain, it may chance of wheat, or of some other grain. But God giveth it a body as it hath pleased Him, and to every seed his own body. All flesh is not the same flesh: but there is one kind of flesh of men, another flesh of beasts, another of fishes, and another of birds. There are also celestial bodies, and bodies terrestrial: but the glory of the celestial is one, and the glory of the terrestrial is another. There is one glory of the sun, and another glory of the moon, and another glory of the stars: for one star differeth from another star in glory. So also is the resurrection of the dead. It is sown in corruption; it is raised in incorruption: It is sown in dishonour; it is raised in glory: it is sown in weakness; it is raised in power: It is sown a natural body; it is raised a spiritual body. There is a natural body, and there is a spiritual body. And so it is written, The first man Adam was made a living soul; the last Adam was made a quickening spirit. Howbeit that was not first which is spiritual, but that which is natural; and afterward that which is spiritual. The first man is of the earth, earthy: the second man is the Lord from heaven. As is the earthy, such are they also that are earthy: and as is the heavenly, such are they also that are heavenly. And as we have borne the image of the earthy, we shall also bear the image of the heavenly. Now this I say, brethren, that flesh and blood cannot inherit the kingdom of God; neither doth corruption inherit incorruption.*

Still dealing with the argumentative, Paul shows that in nature the seed sown dies to its former existence and becomes the plant, wheat, barley etc, whatever the seed was in the first place. As there are different types of flesh, so there are different types of bodies, earthly and heavenly, both different, and with different purposes. Our earthly body then, is sown in corruption, the weakness of the flesh that we have inherited from Adam, and then it is raised in incorruption in Christ the last Adam, Who was the quickening (= who makes alive) spirit. There is [35]another body to come for us, and at the Lord's coming we shall receive it, for our present earthly body cannot contain the glory that is prepared for us, it being corrupt as descending from Adam.

1 Corinthians 15: 51-58: *Behold, I shew you a mystery; We shall not all sleep, but we shall all be changed, In a moment, in the twinkling of an eye, at the last trump: for the trumpet shall sound, and the dead shall be raised incorruptible, and we shall be changed. For this corruptible must put on incorruption, and this mortal must put on immortality. So when this corruptible shall have put on incorruption, and this mortal shall have put on immortality, then shall be brought to pass the saying that is written, Death is swallowed up in victory. O death, where is thy sting? O grave, where is thy victory? The sting of death is sin; and the strength of sin is the law. But thanks be to God, which giveth us the victory through our Lord Jesus Christ. Therefore, my beloved brethren, be ye stedfast, unmoveable, always abounding in the work of the Lord, forasmuch as ye know that your labour is not in vain in the Lord.*

This is the wonderful hope of the Church, that at the Lord's coming we shall be taken up with Him in the way Paul

---

35. See also Philippians 3:20-21 "Who shall change our vile body…"

describes. For those alive at the time it will be "in a moment, in the twinkling of an eye, at the last trump". There are questions about what exactly this last trump is, for some relate it to the Jewish [36]feast of trumpets, and others to the last trump sounded by the [37]angel of revelation. As the feast of trumpets is not relevant to the mainly Gentile believers that Paul is addressing here, and as he does not mention it, I would suggest that the last trump of Revelation, the last trumpet of scripture, is the one Paul refers to, which is the signal for the Lord's coming for His Church. Note that the dead rise first, those who have died believing in the Lord's resurrection, followed by those remaining, hopefully us, who are alive when this event occurs. We shall then be changed, that is, we shall receive our heavenly body as the dead have received theirs, and we shall all be taken up together. This is the victory over death, and over the law, which served to strengthen sin.

Paul finishes this letter with the words "If any man love not the Lord Jesus Christ, let him be anathema. Maranatha", which is no doubt his answer to those who contest the gospel: 'Anathema' (= excommunication), and 'Maranatha' (= our Lord is coming, or has come). Paul is probably referring to the fact that [38]these will be cut off when He comes.

---

36. Numbers 29:1, now Rosh Hoshanna, the blowing of the trumpets (= rams horns, 100 times), originally a one day feast, now two. Relates to the Jewish New Year in September.

37. Revelation 11:15.

38. Hymaneus and Alexander were two people given up to Satan by Paul for opposing the faith. Probably the resurrection doctrines. 1 Tim 1:20, 2 Tim 4:14-15.

CHAPTER SEVEN

PAUL'S LETTERS TO THESSALONICA AND TIMOTHY

❋

1 Thessalonians 1:1–10: *Paul, and Silvanus, and Timotheus, unto the church of the Thessalonians which is in God the Father and in the Lord Jesus Christ: Grace be unto you, and peace, from God our Father, and the Lord Jesus Christ. We give thanks to God always for you all, making mention of you in our prayers; Remembering without ceasing your work of faith, and labour of love, and patience of hope in our Lord Jesus Christ, in the sight of God and our Father; Knowing, brethren beloved, your election of God. For our gospel came not unto you in word only, but also in power, and in the Holy Ghost, and in much assurance; as ye know what manner of men we were among you for your sake. And ye became followers of us, and of the Lord, having received the Word in much affliction, with joy of the Holy Ghost: So that ye were ensamples to all that believe in Macedonia and Achaia. For from you sounded out the Word of the Lord not only in Macedonia and Achaia, but also in every place your faith to God-ward is spread abroad; so that we need not to speak any thing. For they themselves shew of us what manner of entering in we had unto you, and how ye turned to God from idols to serve the living and true God; And to wait for His Son from heaven, Whom He raised from the dead, even Jesus, which delivered us from the wrath to come.*

This church had already heard and known the teachings concerning the last days (a loose term to describe events around the Lord's reappearance, both for His Church, and His nation), and they had received it in their hearts – despite the obvious opposition and affliction that was present at the time. Furthermore, their faith had affected others, and the fellowship they shared was so beneficial that Paul needed to do little except keep an eye on things. Notice that he comments on their "work of faith, labour of love, and patience of hope in our Lord Jesus Christ". This is the example that they set for others, of a church waiting patiently for their Lord to come. This is not without its problems, and not as easy as it may sound, but it is an experience that is attainable for any Christian church. Paul's purpose in writing was to make sure that those things that he had taught them initially would not be lost, despite the efforts of some to introduce doubt through erroneous teaching. He then sums up with the two great points we should pay attention to:

a) We are to "wait for His Son from heaven", and

b) We are "delivered from the wrath to come". We will see, in the next few chapters of these great letters, exactly what Paul meant.

1 Thessalonians 2:1-20: *For yourselves, brethren, know our entrance in unto you, that it was not in vain: But even after that we had suffered before, and were shamefully entreated, as ye know, at Philippi, we were bold in our God to speak unto you the gospel of God with much contention. For our exhortation was not of deceit, nor of uncleanness, nor in guile: But as we were allowed of God to be put in trust with the gospel, even so we speak; not as pleasing men, but God, which trieth*

our hearts. For neither at any time used we flattering words, as ye know, nor a cloke of covetousness; God is witness: Nor of men sought we glory, neither of you, nor yet of others, when we might have been burdensome, as the apostles of Christ. But we were gentle among you, even as a nurse cherisheth her children: So being affectionately desirous of you, we were willing to have imparted unto you, not the gospel of God only, but also our own souls, because ye were dear unto us. For ye remember, brethren, our labour and travail: for labouring night and day, because we would not be chargeable unto any of you, we preached unto you the gospel of God. Ye are witnesses, and God also, how holily and justly and unblameably we behaved ourselves among you that believe: As ye know how we exhorted and comforted and charged every one of you, as a father doth his children, That ye would walk worthy of God, Who hath called you unto His kingdom and glory. For this cause also thank we God without ceasing, because, when ye received the Word of God which ye heard of us, ye received it not as the word of men, but as it is in truth, the Word of God, which effectually worketh also in you that believe. For ye, brethren, became followers of the Churches of God which in Judaea are in Christ Jesus: for ye also have suffered like things of your own countrymen, even as they have of the Jews: Who both killed the Lord Jesus, and their own prophets, and have persecuted us; and they please not God, and are contrary to all men: Forbidding us to speak to the Gentiles that they might be saved, to fill up their sins alway: for the wrath is come upon them to the uttermost. But we, brethren, being taken from you for a short time in presence, not in heart, endeavoured the more abundantly to see your face with great desire. Wherefore we would have come unto you, even I Paul, once and again; but Satan hindered us. For what is our hope, or joy, or crown of rejoicing? Are not even ye in the presence of our Lord Jesus Christ at His coming? For ye are our glory and joy.

Although it is not said here, it is evident that when Paul preached to them the 'Gospel of God' he also taught them about the Lord's coming for them, so it is safe to conclude that all these teachings come under the heading of the Gospel – part of the good news of God, and the Word of God, concerning His Son.

They were not left in ignorance of these truths, as many believers are today, but were taught them right from the start, as a part of their basic induction into the world of faith. It is this complete understanding that they had which drew such opposition against them, for their understanding was affecting others so positively that Paul could say they were his "hope, joy, and crown of rejoicing", his glory and joy to be revealed when the Lord comes.

1 Thessalonians 3:1-13: *Wherefore when we could no longer forbear, we thought it good to be left at Athens alone; And sent Timotheus, our brother, and minister of God, and our fellowlabourer in the gospel of Christ, to establish you, and to comfort you concerning your faith: That no man should be moved by these afflictions: for yourselves know that we are appointed thereunto. For verily, when we were with you, we told you before that we should suffer tribulation; even as it came to pass, and ye know. For this cause, when I could no longer forbear, I sent to know your faith, lest by some means the tempter have tempted you, and our labour be in vain. But now when Timotheus came from you unto us, and brought us good tidings of your faith and charity, and that ye have good remembrance of us always, desiring greatly to see us, as we also to see you: Therefore, brethren, we were comforted over you in all our affliction and distress by your faith: For now we live, if ye stand fast in the Lord. For what thanks can we render to God again for you, for all the joy wherewith we joy for your sakes before our God; Night and day praying exceedingly that we might see your face, and might perfect that*

which is lacking in your faith? Now God Himself and our Father, and our Lord Jesus Christ, direct our way unto you. And the Lord make you to increase and abound in love one toward another, and toward all men, even as we do toward you: To the end He may stablish your hearts unblameable in holiness before God, even our Father, at the coming of our Lord Jesus Christ with all His saints.

Paul's comfort in hearing about them from Timothy was in their 'faith and charity', the two indicators that he always looked for in his charges. Where these are not present together there should be cause for concern, for divisions are the sign of the enemy at work. Paul realised that they were still keen to see him, and recognised they had not been moved by the reports they had heard concerning his tribulations, or problems. At the end of each chapter, Paul draws their attention to a particular aspect of the Lord's coming, and here it reads: "And the dead in Christ shall rise first". There is no reason to suppose that these saints that rise are all what we would call Christians, for this is a later term used to describe believers. The condition seems to be those whose hearts are "unblameable in holiness before God, even our Father, at the coming of our Lord Jesus Christ with all His saints." Who exactly these saints are is not stated, but clearly none are to be left behind at this appearing.

Paul also later states (1 Thessalonians 4:16): "And the dead who are in Christ". This is likely to include all the righteous who have died believing God's record of His Son, Whose appearance was yet future to most of them. If we remind ourselves what Paul said about Abraham in Romans, we see that the 'Church' is more inclusive than we might otherwise have thought, Abraham is considered the 'Father of all them that believe' (Romans 4:11 and 4:20-25) because of his faith, and so those that come with the Lord, His saints, are going to be from various types of backgrounds.

The mystery revealed to Paul concerned the fact that salvation was opened out to the world directly, even to those that were not under the law. It did not depend on adherence to any Jewish traditions concerning the Kingdom Gospel, (that is, of God's people being established on the earth as the spokesmen for God to the world) but was open to all.

1 Thessalonians 4:1-18: *Furthermore then we beseech you, brethren, and exhort you by the Lord Jesus, that as ye have received of us how ye ought to walk and to please God, so ye would abound more and more. For ye know what commandments we gave you by the Lord Jesus. For this is the will of God, even your sanctification, that ye should abstain from fornication: That every one of you should know how to possess his vessel in sanctification and honour; Not in the lust of concupiscence, even as the Gentiles which know not God: That no man go beyond and defraud his brother in any matter: because that the Lord is the avenger of all such, as we also have forewarned you and testified. For God hath not called us unto uncleanness, but unto holiness. He therefore that despiseth, despiseth not man, but God, Who hath also given unto us His Holy Spirit.*

But as touching brotherly love ye need not that I write unto you: for ye yourselves are taught of God to love one another. And indeed ye do it toward all the brethren which are in all Macedonia: but we beseech you, brethren, that ye increase more and more; And that ye study to be quiet, and to do your own business, and to work with your own hands, as we commanded you; That ye may walk honestly toward them that are without, and that ye may have lack of nothing. But I would not have you to be ignorant, brethren, concerning them which are asleep, that ye sorrow not, even as others which have no hope. For if we believe that

Jesus died and rose again, even so them also which sleep in Jesus will God bring with Him. For this we say unto you by the Word of the Lord, that we which are alive and remain unto the coming of the Lord shall not prevent them which are asleep. For the Lord Himself shall descend from heaven with a shout, with the voice of the archangel, and with the trump of God: and the dead in Christ shall rise first: Then we which are alive and remain shall be caught up together with them in the clouds, to meet the Lord in the air: and so shall we ever be with the Lord. Wherefore comfort one another with these words.

Paul's message then is really just a warning of the dangers of fornication, and about defrauding your brother, for he knows that in the past, these were ways by which idolatry and division had entered in. The other thing, brotherly love, which he had intended to speak about, is not said, for *ye yourselves are taught of God to love one another.* There is not a great list of dos and don'ts for these people, simply advice on how to maintain their experience, going over things that they had previously been shown, in order to strengthen them. His real concern is for their understanding concerning the Lord's coming for them and the other Churches, and of His other coming later in judgement for the Jews and unbelievers. The condition for salvation is clearly laid out here: *for if we believe that Jesus died and rose again, even so them also which sleep in Jesus, will God bring with Him.*

Paul showed that if they believed in the resurrection through Jesus Christ, they would also be partakers of it. This by no means excludes those who are already dead and who also have believed. He explains this to them because they are beginning to have doubts about the ones that have died waiting for the Lord, particularly those they knew. This is his reason for writing to them, not to establish these things for the first time, because they already knew them, but rather to explain certain points for them, things that were being challenged by the opposition. It is fortunate for us that this happened, because otherwise we would not have had the privilege of hearing what he had to say about such issues. Here we have written down for us, what Paul had previously only taught by mouth!

Here then, is all we need to know about the Lord's coming for us:

1 Thessalonians 4:15: *For this we say unto you by the Word of the Lord, that we which are alive and remain unto the coming of the Lord shall not prevent them which are asleep.*

The word prevent here is *phthano,* which means to precede or go before, so the living are not going first, the dead will, but only just. 1 Thessalonians 4:16:

For the Lord Himself shall descend from heaven with a shout, with the voice of the archangel, and with the trump of God: and the dead in Christ shall rise first...

We have to be careful here, for it does not state that the Lord will come to earth, although He does come out from heaven, with a shout, the voice of the archangel (Michael), and with the trump of God (the 'last trump, from earlier considerations) and then the 'dead in Christ' (all of them) shall rise first.

1 Thessalonians 4:17: *Then we which are alive and remain shall be caught up together with them in the clouds, to meet the Lord in the air: and so shall we ever be with the Lord.*

There is no indication here of whether the Lord comes to the earth or not, but if He does, we will be with Him, as well as those that have died in Him. For all intents and purposes this is all we need to know about the Lord's coming for us! Which is why Paul says in 1 Thessalonians 4:18: "Wherefore comfort one another with these words." Paul now begins to talk to them about the 'times and seasons', which the Thessalonians understood as the reference to the Jewish experience of the end days. This expression was used by the Lord in Acts 1:6-7:

When they therefore were come together, they asked of Him, saying, Lord wilt Thou at this time restore again the kingdom to Israel? And He said unto them, it is not for you to know the times or the seasons, which the Father has put in His own power.

We should not therefore confuse what applies to the Jewish nation in the last days with what Paul had just written to the Church. The apostles were expecting the restoration of the 'Kingdom' and before this comes the 'Day of the Lord', which is His coming in judgement. Our hope as Christians is of the rapture, of being taken up from the earth to be with the Lord. Paul writes, not to teach new things, but to counteract the erroneous teachings being spread around, which were designed to obscure the simplicity of what he had originally taught. A comparison of what is written will show they are two different subjects. The Church is taught to be ready, to be aware, while the Jews' expectation of the Lord's appearance for them could be at any time:

1 Thessalonians 5:1-3: *But of the times and the seasons, brethren, ye have no need that I write unto you. For yourselves know perfectly that*

the day of the Lord so cometh as a thief in the night. For when they shall say, Peace and safety; then sudden destruction cometh upon them, as travail upon a woman with child; and they shall not escape.

The peace and safety here, is [39]possibly the celebration of an agreement between Arab and Jew, the signing of the treaty that marks the beginning of sorrows and the great tribulation periods. Where most nations are concerned this could be the breakthrough that heralds peace – everyone can now go about their own business, and concentrate on their own national welfare. What they do not appreciate is that this could mark the beginning of the last week, the beginning of the judgements of the Lord, and then of God Himself.

1 Thessalonians 5:4-10: *But ye, brethren, are not in darkness, that that day should overtake you as a thief. Ye are all the children of light, and the children of the day: we are not of the night, nor of darkness. Therefore let us not sleep, as do others; but let us watch and be sober. For they that sleep sleep in the night; and they that be drunken are drunken in the night. But let us, who are of the day, be sober, putting on the breastplate of faith and love; and for an helmet, the hope of salvation. For God hath not appointed us to wrath, but to obtain salvation by our Lord Jesus Christ, Who died for us, that, whether we wake or sleep, we should live together with Him.*

The darkness is for the world; non-believers, whether Jew or Gentile, but for us, being the children of the light, we are unaffected by these later events, as we are not appointed to wrath. It is unlikely that we will be around for the worst of these

---

39. It could also be the world's celebration of the death of the two witnesses, 3½ years later, which precedes the second part of the week, the period of great tribulation. Rev 11:10 (torment = to test, try, as proving gold or metals, to inflict pain).

events, although it is by no means certain when exactly we shall be taken. We are expected to be awake and aware of the times, but whether we are alive or dead when He comes will not affect our status in the Lord. He will come for us anyway.

1 Thessalonians 5:11: *Wherefore comfort yourselves together, and edify one another, even as also ye do.*

It is unlikely that these words would be much comfort to the Church if Paul were preparing them to go through the great tribulation. His point here is to show that these judgements are not for believers, who have already confessed and forsaken their sins and have been forgiven. The judgement is for those who have rejected God's record of His Son through His Word.

1 Thessalonians 5:12-28: *And we beseech you, brethren, to know them which labour among you, and are over you in the Lord, and admonish you; And to esteem them very highly in love for their work's sake. And be at peace among yourselves. Now we exhort you, brethren, warn them that are unruly, comfort the feebleminded, support the weak, be patient toward all men. See that none render evil for evil unto any man; but ever follow that which is good, both among yourselves, and to all men. Rejoice evermore. Pray without ceasing. In every thing give thanks: for this is the will of God in Christ Jesus concerning you. Quench not the Spirit. Despise not prophesyings. Prove all things; hold fast that which is good. Abstain from all appearance of evil. And the very God of peace sanctify you wholly; and I pray God your whole spirit and soul and body be preserved blameless unto the coming of our Lord Jesus Christ. Faithful is He that calleth you, Who also will do it. Brethren, pray for us. Greet all the brethren with an holy kiss. I charge you by the Lord that this epistle be read unto all the holy brethren. The grace of our Lord Jesus Christ be with you. Amen.*

In the light of the Lord's coming, Paul's exhortation is for them is to continue with their fellowship in all of these teachings, allowing the Holy Spirit to minister without hindrance, and to share these truths with others. The teachings concerning the Lord's coming for the Church, His *parousia,* or the rapture, as we call it, and the truths concerning the 'Day of the Lord', and the 'times and the seasons' are all basic teachings that should be [40]shared.

2 Thessalonians 1:1-12: *Paul, and Silvanus, and Timotheus, unto the Church of the Thessalonians in God our Father and the Lord Jesus Christ: Grace unto you, and peace, from God our Father and the Lord Jesus Christ. We are bound to thank God always for you, brethren, as it is meet, because that your faith groweth exceedingly, and the charity of every one of you all toward each other aboundeth; So that we ourselves glory in you in the Churches of God for your patience and faith in all your persecutions and tribulations that ye endure: Which is a manifest token of the righteous judgment of God, that ye may be counted worthy of the kingdom of God, for which ye also suffer: Seeing it is a righteous thing with God to recompense tribulation to them that trouble you; And to you who are troubled rest with us, when the Lord Jesus shall be revealed from heaven with His mighty angels, In flaming fire taking vengeance on them that know not God, and that obey not the gospel of our Lord Jesus Christ: Who shall be punished with everlasting destruction from the presence of the Lord, and from the glory of His power; When He shall come to be glorified in His saints, and to be admired in all them that believe (because our testimony among you was believed) in that day. Wherefore also we pray always for you, that our God would count you worthy of this calling, and fulfil all the good*

---

40. Although these things can be complex and mysterious to us, the real meaning of the Greek 'apocalypse' (ie: The book of Revelation) is of a mystery revealed, something opened out, rather than something kept secret. The scriptures are written for us, to be understood by any who seek to know the truth.

pleasure of His goodness, and the work of faith with power: That the name of our Lord Jesus Christ may be glorified in you, and ye in Him, according to the grace of our God and the Lord Jesus Christ.

Once again, faith and charity are the indicators of spiritual health that Paul looked for when he considered the state of the churches. He found in the Thessalonians that there was an abundance of both despite the [41]persecutions and tribulations they endured. The antidote to suffering was patience and faith, itself the manifest token of the righteous judgement of God. In other words, God would also wait and be patient, until the time comes to manifest His judgements on the world of unbelief, and the persecutors of His people. According to 2 Thessalonians 1:7-10, this comes:

…when the Lord Jesus shall be revealed from heaven with His mighty angels, In flaming fire taking vengeance on them that know not God, and that obey not the gospel of our Lord Jesus Christ: Who shall be punished with everlasting destruction from the presence of the Lord, and from the glory of His power; When He shall come to be glorified in His saints, and to be admired in all them that believe (because our testimony among you was believed) in that day.

Again it is important to consider what is said here, for we could easily conclude from reading this that our part is with the Jews, in the later kingdom, for the Lord's coming in this instance is in judgement. But Paul is saying to the Thessalonians that they should have 'rest with us' when this happens, that is, that they are not part of it, their recompense for the tribulations they are suffering is to be in rest, and they will then be with the Lord and Paul.

---

41. Being pursued and put under pressure, this would seem to be in regard to the doctrines they held.

The coming that he now refers to is a different, and later, coming of the Lord, when all things shall be balanced and judged, and when the Lord is *revealed from heaven with His mighty angels*. His coming for the Church is not described in such language, neither is it stated that the Lord is revealed to others when He comes for us. Paul is saying that the judgement of the world is deferred to that later time, during and after the time of great tribulation, which although specific to Israel, will also draw in and include the whole world, especially those that worship the Beast!

2 Thessalonians 2:1-17: *Now we beseech you, brethren, by the coming of our Lord Jesus Christ, and by our gathering together unto Him, That ye be not soon shaken in mind, or be troubled, neither by spirit, nor by word, nor by letter as from us, as that the day of Christ is at hand. Let no man deceive you by any means: for that day shall not come, except there come a falling away first, and that man of sin be revealed, the son of perdition; Who opposeth and exalteth himself above all that is called God, or that is worshipped; so that he as God sitteth in the temple of God, shewing himself that he is God. Remember ye not, that, when I was yet with you, I told you these things? And now ye know what withholdeth that he might be revealed in His time. For the mystery of iniquity doth already work: only He Who now letteth will let, until he be taken out of the way. And then shall that Wicked be revealed, whom the Lord shall consume with the spirit of His mouth, and shall destroy with the brightness of His coming: Even him, whose coming is after the working of Satan with all power and signs and lying wonders, And with all deceivableness of unrighteousness in them that perish; because they received not the love of the truth, that they might be saved. And for this cause God shall send them strong delusion, that they should believe a lie: That they all might be damned who believed not the truth, but had*

pleasure in unrighteousness. But we are bound to give thanks alway to God for you, brethren beloved of the Lord, because God hath from the beginning chosen you to salvation through sanctification of the Spirit and belief of the truth: Whereunto He called you by our gospel, to the obtaining of the glory of our Lord Jesus Christ. Therefore, brethren, stand fast, and hold the traditions which ye have been taught, whether by word, or our epistle. Now our Lord Jesus Christ Himself, and God, even our Father, which hath loved us, and hath given us everlasting consolation and good hope through grace, Comfort your hearts, and stablish you in every good word and work.

Here are the problems that this church is being given, the result of the persecutions and tribulation brought by some, who are now inferring that these people have missed the Lord's coming. He brings them straight to these doctrines of the Lord's coming *(parousia)* and of our gathering together unto Him *(episunagoge* – gathering together in one place), assuring them that the '[42]day of Christ' (which is wrongly translated here, and should read the 'Day of the Lord') would not come unless certain conditions are met, namely:

2 Thessalonians 2:3-4: *...for that day shall not come, except there come a [43]falling away first, and that man of sin be revealed, the son of perdition; Who opposeth and exalteth himself above all that is called God, or that is worshipped; so that he as God sitteth in the temple of God, shewing himself that he is God.*

His revealing, which Paul had already talked to them about, comes when Satan is cast out of heaven and empowers the Beast,

---

42. Philippians 1:10 refers to this day, when the Lord comes for believers. This is not subject to any conditions, there does not have to be a falling away first, or the man of sin be revealed. It could come at any time.

43. Note that this refers to the revealing of the 'man of sin' and is not relevant to the church. Paul wrote that the 'fulness of the Gentiles' would come, in Romans 11:25, this is an adding to

or man of sin, to fulfil his real role as the deceiver of the earth. Satan meanwhile is holding fast, at this time, to his place in the heavens, but the inevitable will occur, and he will be [44]removed from his current place of authority. Of course, those who believe what is written in the Word may well spot 'the beast' before this, as the one who promotes the seven-year deal with Israel that will include the ability to worship on the sacred site of the temple mount. But it is not certain that he will be generally known until he makes his move, later on, towards Israel. Those who are deceived by the Beast can look forward to the judgements of God, but Paul was really showing these believers that none of this had happened yet, so that they did not need to be concerned about what others were writing, saying in the gifts of the Spirit, misquoting from scripture, or otherwise ministering to them. The point is they had not missed the Lord's coming for them.

Paul's concern for these believers is that they might alter their path and let go of the original teachings because of the false ones, thereby weakening and jeopardising their experience. They had it right in the first place, and this is why they were coming under spiritual attack; it was the opposition to the doctrines and truths they held. This is a particular lesson for those of us who are seeking the truth in these days, for we are very much closer to the end than in the time of Paul. To have the truth, and hold onto it, will make us a target for Satan, for such believers are a threat to him. We do not have to do anything to provoke such opposition, we merely make our stand in the truth, and attempts will be made to move us from it. Whether this is by way of inner doubts and questions concerning what we know, or by teaching from outside, which may appear more

44. Rev 12:7-17, cast out by the angel that previously could not rebuke him (ref: Jude) Michael.

palatable or scholarly, it will surely come in some form or other. There is an abundance of information available instantly on the Internet which contains elements of truth to give it some form of credibility but *is* misleading in its end. Central to our salvation are the doctrines of the Lord's resurrection, and of our own resurrection in Him. If this can be weakened, by convincing us that we are yet to be judged with the world, then fear and doubt will set in. [45]*Buy the truth, and sell it not* is excellent advice for us in these dangerous times, and we should never underestimate either the power of the Word that we hold fast to or the lengths to which Satan will go in order to rob us of it. His efforts to move us from the truth should be taken as evidence of its value.

Paul finishes this epistle with some practical advice that is necessary for them:

2 Thessalonians 3:1–12: *Finally, brethren, pray for us, that the Word of the Lord may have free course, and be glorified, even as it is with you: And that we may be delivered from unreasonable and wicked men: for all men have not faith. But the Lord is faithful, Who shall stablish you, and keep you from evil. And we have confidence in the Lord touching you, that ye both do and will do the things which we command you. And the Lord direct your hearts into the love of God, and into the patient waiting for Christ. Now we command you, brethren, in the name of our Lord Jesus Christ, that ye withdraw yourselves from every brother that walketh disorderly, and not after the tradition which he received of us. For yourselves know how ye ought to follow us: for we behaved not ourselves disorderly among you; Neither did we eat any man's bread for nought; but wrought with labour and travail night and day, that we might not be chargeable to any of you: Not because we have not power,*

45. Proverbs 23:23.

but to make ourselves an ensample unto you to follow us. For even when we were with you, this we commanded you, that if any would not work, neither should he eat. For we hear that there are some which walk among you disorderly, working not at all, but are busybodies. Now them that are such we command and exhort by our Lord Jesus Christ, that with quietness they work, and eat their own bread.

The ones causing the trouble within could well be those *walking disorderly* having too much time on their hands and displaying too much interest in what others are doing in their own spiritual lives. Paul is not advocating that this, or any other church, should be a social service, as clearly these people are perfectly capable of working but will not, being more interested in passing on their own opinions to those others who are too polite to resist them.

The time had come for this to be put to an end in Thessalonica, and from then on, they would have to be more particular about their fellowship, and consider what it was costing them to listen to such people, who are so out of step with what Paul taught. He does not advocate that these be put out of the Church as yet, rather that they be made aware that their opinions and company are not welcome until they start to concentrate on their own relationship with the Lord. The Thessalonians are to admonish (or gently warn) all those who would promote doctrines other than those they had received. Paul's signature was the proof of his authorship, and they were to be cautious about anything presented to them, which didn't have this.

2 Thessalonians 3:13-18: *But ye, brethren, be not weary in well doing. And if any man obey not our word by this epistle, note that man, and have no company with him, that he may be ashamed. Yet count him not*

as an enemy, but admonish him as a brother. Now the Lord of peace Himself give you peace always by all means. The Lord be with you all. The salutation of Paul with mine own hand, which is the token in every epistle: so I write. The grace of our Lord Jesus Christ be with you all. Amen. The second epistle to the Thessalonians was written from Athens.

1 Timothy 4:1-11: *Now the Spirit speaketh expressly, that in the latter times some shall depart from the faith, giving heed to seducing spirits, and doctrines of devils; Speaking lies in hypocrisy; having their conscience seared with a hot iron; Forbidding to marry, and commanding to abstain from meats, which God hath created to be received with thanksgiving of them which believe and know the truth. For every creature of God is good, and nothing to be refused, if it be received with thanksgiving: For it is sanctified by the Word of God and prayer. If thou put the brethren in remembrance of these things, thou shalt be a good minister of Jesus Christ, nourished up in the words of faith and of good doctrine, whereunto thou hast attained. But refuse profane and old wives' fables, and exercise thyself rather unto godliness. For bodily exercise profiteth little: but godliness is profitable unto all things, having promise of the life that now is, and of that which is to come. This is a faithful saying and worthy of all acceptation. For therefore we both labour and suffer reproach, because we trust in the living God, Who is the Saviour of all men, specially of those that believe. These things command and teach.*

Paul shows that the ministry of the Holy Spirit was being used to strengthen believers of the time regarding those that were falling away from the truth Equally, other spirits were attempting to replace the Gospel teachings with doctrines that were essentially demonic. There seems to be a willingness for these false teachers to be used in such a way, cutting off the voice of their own conscience and denying what they must have been taught themselves, in order to dominate and control the faith of others. Forbidding marriage and controlling diet seem to be the focus of their doctrine, directly contrary to bible teaching which, after the flood, allowed for a change in the diet to include meat. Vegetarianism and vegan practice have flourished over the last twenty years, and the culture of the gym and the body beautiful has also made most of us appear somewhat lacking physically. Paul summed this up under the heading 'profane and old wives' fables', and as far as he was concerned there were no restrictions on believers regarding this at all. Where some seek to control what we eat, whom we see and whether or not we exercise, we should be rightly cautious, for the inspiration behind this form of control comes from spiritual beings.

2 Timothy 3:1-17: *This know also, that in the last days perilous times shall come. For men shall be lovers of their own selves, covetous, boasters, proud, blasphemers, disobedient to parents, unthankful, unholy, Without natural affection, trucebreakers, false accusers, incontinent, fierce, despisers of those that are good, Traitors, heady, highminded, lovers of pleasures more than lovers of God; Having a form of godliness, but denying the power thereof: from such turn away. For of this sort are they which creep into houses, and lead captive silly women laden with sins, led away with divers lusts, Ever learning, and never able to come to the knowledge of the truth. Now as Jannes and Jambres withstood Moses, so do these also resist the truth: men of corrupt minds, reprobate concerning the faith. But they shall proceed no further: for their folly shall be manifest unto all men, as their's also was.*

But thou hast fully known my doctrine, manner of life, purpose, faith, longsuffering, charity, patience, Persecutions, afflictions, which came unto me at Antioch, at Iconium, at Lystra; what persecutions I endured: but out of them all the Lord delivered me. Yea, and all that will live godly in Christ Jesus shall suffer persecution. But evil men and seducers shall wax worse and worse, deceiving, and being deceived. But continue thou in the things which thou hast learned and hast been assured of, knowing of Whom thou hast learned them; And that from a child thou hast known the holy scriptures, which are able to make thee wise unto salvation through faith which is in Christ Jesus. All scripture is given by inspiration of God, and is profitable for doctrine, for reproof, for correction, for instruction in righteousness: That the man of God may be perfect, throughly furnished unto all good works.

Paul's words here should not be ignored as they are particularly relevant to us in these last times, and clearly *some will depart from the faith.* Sin is not a new thing by any means, but we are warned that mankind in general, and people who claim to know God, in particular, will be the cause of troubles for those trying to hold on to their experience of faith. The Greek word used here *chalepos*, translated 'perilous', means difficult or hard to bear, with the idea of wearing down, or weakening. The explanation of this is in the prevailing attitudes that we may encounter:

2 Timothy 3:2-5:

"lovers of their own selves, (selfish)

covetous, (lovers of money)

boasters, (an empty pretender)

proud, (despising others)

blasphemers, (speaking evil against God or man)

disobedient to parents, (not compliant)

unthankful, (ungrateful)

unholy, (wicked)

Without natural affection (hard hearted towards family/brethren)

Trucebreakers, (truceless, who cannot be persuaded to agree)

false accusers, (slanderer, wicked)

incontinent, (without self control)

fierce, (savage, untameable)

despisers of those that are good (hostile to virtue),

Traitors, (surrendering to the enemy, helping him)

heady, (falling headlong, rash)

highminded, (enveloped in smoke, puffed up)

lovers of pleasures more than lovers of God; (love of pleasure greater than of God)

Having a form of godliness, but denying the power thereof: (The appearance of godliness, the outward form, but not subject to the power of god))

from such turn away.

Let's be realistic here, and accept that some of these traits are going to be found among us. We are fleshly, and these are attributes of the flesh so there is very little we can do about it. What is pertinent though is that some who may profess to be believers are going to be the cause of these attitudes being introduced into communities of believers, to their detriment. It is those to whom we may have previous connections, associations or history who may attempt to influence us, and this is why it is a danger. There are, and will continue to be, those whose motives are selfish, having an alternative agenda that owes more to the flesh than to the spirit. They will be amongst Christian believers in the same way that the false teachers of which the Lord warned us will be amongst the latter-day Jew.

For many of us, the pathway to the truth has already involved running a gauntlet of such people, who have made what was intended to be a simple and uncomplicated experience into a minefield of mistrust, causing us at times to question what the truth really is. Praise is due to the Lord here, for [46] *The Lord knoweth them that are His* and is [47] *able to save them to the uttermost that come unto God by Him,* for by His grace we can survive. Perhaps it is the place of them who know these things to warn those who do not, in pointing out what the depths of the opposition can involve in these last times. By and large the motives of these people are sexual, financial, or both, and in some instances include a desire to gain respect or adulation for themselves through controlling others.

The danger is in how genuine they can appear, and the unwary can easily be fooled:

2 Timothy 3:6-7: *For of this sort are they which creep into houses, and lead captive silly women laden with sins, led away with divers lusts, Ever learning, and never able to come to the knowledge of the truth.*

Neither should we be dismissive of the methods used, for, according to 2 Timothy 3:8-9: *as Jannes and Jambres withstood Moses, so do these also resist the truth: men of corrupt minds, reprobate concerning the faith. But they shall proceed no further: for their folly shall be manifest unto all men, as theirs also was.*

At first the signs and teachings these produce are extremely convincing, being able to duplicate the truth to a degree, for as Satan appears as a minister of light, so his operatives may use the

46. 2 Tim 2:19.
47. Hebrews 7:25.

scriptures as he did, to add authenticity to their claims. This has a limited life however, for in His time the Lord will show the limits to which they can deceive, and their works will be manifest for what they are. We have to trust the Lord that the damage they appear to do is not lasting, and that those who seek Him, whilst having their faith tried, are not finally lost. Paul's claim to true apostleship was his own lifestyle and approach, and they could look to him for an example of how the Lord's ministers should behave. Anyone following the Lord fully should demonstrate the following attributes; a life lived in the Lord should contain all of these things.

2 Timothy 3:10-12: *But thou hast fully known my doctrine, manner of life, purpose, faith, longsuffering, charity, patience, Persecutions, afflictions, which came unto me at Antioch, at Iconium, at Lystra; what persecutions I endured: but out of them all the Lord delivered me. Yea, and all that will live godly in Christ Jesus shall suffer persecution.*

But we can look forward to more of the same resistance to our faith as the time of our Lord's coming draws near. Things will definitely not improve, so we must be aware of what we might face, and be prepared for it.

2 Timothy 3:13-17: *But evil men and seducers shall wax worse and worse, deceiving, and being deceived. But continue thou in the things which thou hast learned, and hast been assured of, knowing of Whom thou hast learned them. And that, from a child thou hast known the holy scriptures, which are able to make thee wise unto salvation through faith which is in Jesus Christ. All scripture is given by inspiration of God, and is profitable for doctrine, for reproof, for correction, for instruction in righteousness. That the man of God may be perfect, throughly furnished unto all good works.*

2 Timothy 4:1-8: *I charge thee therefore before God, and the Lord Jesus Christ, Who shall judge the quick and the dead at His appearing and His kingdom; Preach the Word; be instant in season, out of season; reprove, rebuke, exhort with all longsuffering and doctrine. For the time will come when they will not endure sound doctrine; but after their own lusts shall they heap to themselves teachers, having itching ears; And they shall turn away their ears from the truth, and shall be turned unto fables. But watch thou in all things, endure afflictions, do the work of an evangelist, make full proof of thy ministry. For I am now ready to be offered, and the time of my departure is at hand. I have fought a good fight, I have finished my course, I have kept the faith: Henceforth there is laid up for me a crown of righteousness, which the Lord, the righteous judge, shall give me at that day: and not to me only, but unto all them also that love His appearing.*

Writing in particular to Timothy, in the belief that he might go on to face these things, Paul brings him back to the basics that would see him through, assuring him that the scriptures contain all that is needed for the man of God to prosper, even in these perilous times. Wickedness will increase, and as it does, it will be accepted as normal; this is a spiralling downward trend, as we will no doubt have observed in our own lives. Even in such times, however, there is a provision for anyone who wants to walk with God, and have the fullest experience available. Men or women of God can be perfected through hearing and being guided by the scriptures, as Timothy was.

Although there will not necessarily be a mass exodus from the Church, there will be increasing pressure that is designed to weaken our resolve and compromise ourselves, and that will affect some. The tendency to look for new and strange ideas will be encouraged by the opposition, but the decision to turn their 'ears away from the truth' is ultimately the responsibility of the individual, for sound doctrine is available for those who seek it in God's Word.

It remains that for those that love the Lord's appearing, those who are waiting in faith for Him to come, there is a *crown of righteousness* to go with the crowns of [48]life and of [49]glory that are also available. For this reason alone it is worth pursuing an understanding of what is involved in these last days, for there is an undoubted reward to us for keeping these truths in our hearts until He comes for us.

If we value these things, we are more likely to hold on to them. It is what the Lord wants us to be doing!

48. James 1:12
49. 1 Peter 5:4

CHAPTER EIGHT

THE SEVEN CHURCHES

The Book of Revelation, more properly named the 'Revelation of Jesus Christ,' is the subject of much controversy, both in regard to its authorship and its message. There is no point trying to deal with all the various arguments here, as we will do better to examine what has been written in the book, rather than what has been written about it. The author, both in my view and that of the early Church fathers, was the disciple John, who from his own words "was in the isle that is called Patmos, for the Word of God, and for the testimony of Jesus Christ." This suggests, but does not confirm by any means, that he was in exile on the Isle of Patmos for his continued belief and testimony in the Lord.

The commonly accepted view is that he was about ninety years old at the time, and therefore would have been on Patmos in the last years of the reign of the Emperor Domitian, about 95AD. It is also believed that he was on Patmos for about eighteen months when, according to the custom of some prisoners being freed on the Emperor's death, John was released to go back to Ephesus to end his days as bishop of the churches in Asia. This would make sense, as the book he was about to write was to be distributed to Ephesus, and the six other churches nearby. Paul had written thirty years earlier to Timothy saying that *all those that be in Asia be turned away from me*, and we can be confident that John wrote to a different group of believers. John, or more accurately the Lord, makes no concession towards Paul's gospel of grace or any of the doctrines that he taught, and instead there is a strong Jewish flavour found in the wording of the messages to the Churches of Revelation. Having said that, everything written by Daniel, the Lord, Peter and Paul, can be accommodated within the Book of Revelation. By its very content the main scope of the book must be seen as an instrument for the future Jews of the new Kingdom Gospel that it heralds, which will also be proclaimed by its two witnesses, of which more later.

Revelation 1:1-2: *The Revelation of Jesus Christ, which God gave unto Him, to shew unto His servants things which must shortly come to pass; and He sent and signified it by His angel unto His servant John: Who bare record of the Word of God, and of the testimony of Jesus Christ, and of all things that he saw.*

Clearly we are looking at God's revelation of His Will, but this was specifically given to the Lord, to show unto His servants, through John. This is not going to be [50]understood in general terms except by those to whom it is sent, and who will gladly receive it. We are His sons and yet also His servants in our walk, so it is our place to seek an understanding of these truths, even though they may not directly affect us. It is also worth mentioning that as this revelation is a gift to the Lord from His Father, and therefore something close to His heart, we should treasure it as He does, in order to share in the same blessing. As believers we ignore these truths is to our own detriment.

50. Daniel 12:9-10.

Revelation 1:3: *Blessed is he that readeth, and they that hear the words of this prophecy, and keep those things which are written therein: for the time is at hand.*

Note too that the blessing in the book belongs to those who read, hear and keep those things. For myself, every time I read this book or even parts of it, something new is revealed. I would suggest that the best way to understanding this book (and others in scripture) is to read it over several times, and then allow the Spirit to shed light on it as He will. It may take some time of course, but becoming familiar with it develops into a personal blessing for the reader. The message to the hearers is to take note, for the expectation when it was written was that these things could come upon the world at any time. Subsequent delays must fall within God's plan of grace being worked out for the non-Jewish world, but once this work is complete, the events described will surely start to unfold and the Jewish nation will once again find itself at the centre in God's plan.

Revelation 1:4-9: *John to the seven churches which are in Asia: Grace be unto you, and peace, from Him which is, and which was, and which is to come; and from the seven Spirits which are before His throne; And from Jesus Christ, Who is the faithful witness, and the first begotten of the dead, and the prince of the kings of the earth. Unto Him that loved us, and washed us from our sins in His own blood. And hath made us kings and priests unto God and His Father; to Him be glory and dominion for ever and ever. Amen. Behold, He cometh with clouds; and every eye shall see Him, and they also which pierced Him: and all kindreds of the earth shall wail because of Him. Even so, Amen. I am Alpha and Omega, the beginning and the ending, saith the Lord, which is, and which was, and which is to come, the Almighty. I John, who also am your brother, and companion in tribulation, and in the kingdom and patience of Jesus Christ, was in the isle that is called Patmos, for the Word of God, and for the testimony of Jesus Christ.*

John is clear about what to do with this revelation, for he is told to write specifically to the seven churches around Asia. The Greek word used here, *ecclesia*, simply means those called out, or an assembly, and is used in a very loose sense. It can refer to any group of believers, and does not necessarily point to Gentile believers, those we nowadays refer to as the Church. It was used to describe groups of Jewish believers as well, as is the case here. They are believers, but the terminology is Jewish; they are *kings and priests'* but also servants, in their role. It must be within John's means to get this information across to Asia, and it raises the question – if he were a slave in Patmos, as is widely supposed, how would this be accomplished?

Patmos is not as isolated as we might imagine, being very close to Ephesus, and sea trade to the other islands and mainland would be frequent. Parts of modern-day Turkey can be easily seen from Patmos, as it is so close. John was unlikely to be made to work at his age, although he may have been employed as a scribe. His status alone, as the last living apostle, could have been enough to merit banishment, and it seems likely he was sent out of the way as a precaution, as the imperial cult of Roman emperor worship was revived under Domitian's rule. If he was sent there to be silenced, it manifestly didn't work, as the Lord used John's time there to good effect in revealing to him the whole future of mankind. Clearly John was meant to be there in God's plan, but for what cause and in what capacity, we cannot say with certainty! The preceding words seem to come from John himself as an introduction, and form a summary of what was to come, for John includes the fact that the Lord's coming would be visible to all, especially to that nation which had Him crucified – Israel.

Revelation 1:10-20: *I was in the Spirit on the Lord's day, and heard behind me a great voice, as of a trumpet, Saying, I am Alpha and Omega, the first and the last: and, What thou seest, write in a book, and send it unto the seven churches which are in Asia; unto Ephesus, and unto Smyrna, and unto Pergamos, and unto Thyatira, and unto Sardis, and unto Philadelphia, and unto Laodicea. And I turned to see the voice that spake with me. And being turned, I saw seven golden candlesticks; And in the midst of the seven candlesticks one like unto the Son of Man, clothed with a garment down to the foot, and girt about the paps with a golden girdle. His head and His hairs were white like wool, as white as snow; and His eyes were as a flame of fire; And His feet like unto fine brass, as if they burned in a furnace; and His voice as the sound of many waters. And He had in His right hand seven stars: and out of His mouth went a sharp two-edged sword: and His countenance was as the sun shineth in his strength. And when I saw Him, I fell at His feet as dead. And He laid His right hand upon me, saying unto me, Fear not; I am the first and the last: I am He that liveth, and was dead; and, behold, I am alive for evermore, Amen; and have the keys of hell and of death. Write the things which thou hast seen, and the things which are, and the things which shall be hereafter; The mystery of the seven stars which thou sawest in My right hand, and the seven golden candlesticks. The seven stars are the angels of the seven churches: and the seven candlesticks which thou sawest are the seven churches.*

John is referring to the Day of the Lord, of course, and not our church Sunday. He was about to be shown the sequence of events due to take place in the last prophetic week for Israel, and beyond that. Here is the final explanation, the convergence of all that previous prophets had been shown, and the Lord now expands on those things that He spoke about in the Gospels, to their full extent. His appearance from behind John is dazzling, and John is evidently close, for he falls at His feet, and the Lord lays His hand on him. This takes place on the earth, at Patmos. The explanation is given straightaway of what John sees; first the Lord, and then the seven stars and candlesticks, which are the ministers of the churches, and the churches themselves. It is to the angels of the churches that the messages are to be sent, a different message for each minister, but each church is to see the whole book, containing the things that "thou hast seen, the things which are, and the things which shall be hereafter." In order then, first Ephesus:

Revelation 2:1-7: *Unto the angel of the church of Ephesus write; These things saith He that holdeth the seven stars in His right hand, Who walketh in the midst of the seven golden candlesticks; I know thy works, and thy labour, and thy patience, and how thou canst not bear them which are evil: and thou hast tried them which say they are apostles, and are not, and hast found them liars: And hast borne, and hast patience, and for My name's sake hast laboured, and hast not fainted. Nevertheless I have somewhat against thee, because thou hast left thy first love. Remember therefore from whence thou art fallen, and repent, and do the first works; or else I will come unto thee quickly, and will remove thy candlestick out of his place, except thou repent. But this thou hast, that thou hatest the deeds of the Nicolaitans, which I also hate. He that hath an ear, let him hear what the Spirit saith unto the churches; To him that overcometh will I give to eat of the tree of life, which is in the midst of the paradise of God.*

As in all of these messages there is a reference to the Lord that John saw, and here it is *the First and the Last, which was dead and is alive.* The Lord addresses the *angel of the church,* (*angelos* = messenger, one who brings tidings), the minister at the time, whose duty it was to bring the Lord's Word to the congregation. The message is pertinent to the Church of Ephesus at that specific time, the present state of that church being that they had things that were to their credit, but they also had 'left thy first love', who was the Lord. This He called their first works, and despite any other efforts, they are lacking in the Lord's sight to the extent that they could lose their place in Him, as a church. Their works then, were not enough in the Lord's sight, although they are taken into account in His overall assessment of them. Their lack is in spite of the fact that they have had false teachers amongst them claiming to be apostles, as well as efforts to convince them that the deeds of the Nicolaitans were acceptable, whatever these deeds were. We should question how it could be that they had left the Lord in the midst of this, and my suggestion is that they had become vain in their own spirituality, and because they were wise to the opposition they had faced, had become over confident in their own wisdom, failing to give the Lord the credit for opening their eyes to the truth.

The reward for those who take heed to the message was to *eat of the tree of life* an earthly reward, but referring to the new Jerusalem that is described later, as befitting their place as believing Jews. Notice the condition, and the message of the Spirit is *him that overcometh*, and this is the statement repeated to all the churches. They are expected to overcome their own particular range of difficulties, which differed in each Church, but was in this case to *Remember therefore from whence thou art fallen, and repent, and do the first works.*

Smyrna

Revelation 2:8–11: *And unto the angel of the church in Smyrna write; These things saith the first and the last, which was dead, and is alive; I know thy works, and tribulation, and poverty, (but thou art rich) and I know the blasphemy of them which say they are Jews, and are not, but are the synagogue of Satan. Fear none of those things which thou shalt suffer: behold, the devil shall cast some of you into prison, that ye may be tried; and ye shall have tribulation ten days: be thou faithful unto death, and I will give thee a crown of life. He that hath an ear, let him hear what the Spirit saith unto the churches; He that overcometh shall not be hurt of the second death.*

Here the Lord presents Himself as the one that was dead and is alive, and we can see that this was to be an encouragement for them, as some were to be killed. This could be because of those who were of the 'synagogue of Satan', who may have been Jewish by descent but not by [51]nature. Satan is given the credit for this persecution, and those who were to be cast into prison were to be tormented or tortured for ten days, after which they would receive a crown of life. Probably the greatest suffering would be in having to listen to the blasphemy of their persecutors, and these people were obviously despised being poor, but nevertheless faithful. We are reminded here of [52]Daniel and the Lord's words foretelling the Jews turning on each other, as this has implications for the latter day Jew, who can expect to find a similar form of treachery to come. The second death is later mentioned in Revelation 20:6, and any Jews killed for their faith during the persecutions of the last week will escape this, and will live again in the first resurrection, reigning with Christ in Israel for a thousand years.

51. Romans 2:28-29.
52. Daniel 11:32-35, Mark 13:12.

Pergamos

Revelation 2:12-17: *And to the angel of the church in Pergamos write; These things saith He which hath the sharp sword with two edges; I know thy works, and where thou dwellest, even where Satan's seat is: and thou holdest fast My name, and hast not denied My faith, even in those days wherein Antipas was My faithful martyr, who was slain among you, where Satan dwelleth. But I have a few things against thee, because thou hast there them that hold the doctrine of Balaam, who taught Balac to cast a stumblingblock before the children of Israel, to eat things sacrificed unto idols, and to commit fornication. So hast thou also them that hold the doctrine of the Nicolaitans, which thing I hate. Repent; or else I will come unto thee quickly, and will fight against them with the sword of My mouth. He that hath an ear, let him hear what the Spirit saith unto the churches; To him that overcometh will I give to eat of the hidden manna, and will give him a white stone, and in the stone a new name written, which no man knoweth saving he that receiveth it.*

Our attention is drawn to this church because it is where Satan's seat is said to be. Tradition has it that a temple was built to Zeus here, and the [53]seat referred to was at the top of the altar steps. Within their living [54]memory, Antipas was (publicly?) [55]martyred, and the Lord commends them for not having denied Him in the face of such extreme pressure. It is [56]held that Antipas was a dentist, as well as being bishop of the Church, and that he resisted the official line that health and social care was at the provision of the Roman authorities, and therefore access depended upon partaking of sacrifices to official gods.

53. This is the altar that was excavated and taken to a Museum in Berlin in 1901, and is still there.
54. 92AD
55. Said to have been roasted inside a brass bull, these contained complicated tubes to emulate bull's voices.
56. But cannot be proved!

Domitian revived the practice of the Imperial cult, considering himself a god, and any non-compliance or resistance may have been the cause of [57]Antipas being killed. Pergamos also contained a temple to Aesculapius, a renowned centre of healing. We cannot be certain of the real truth now, but what we do know from scripture is that this church is not perfect, having both those that hold the doctrine of Balaam, (who considered that having an experience with God could be used for personal gain) and the Nicolaitans (meaning 'power over the people', who also offended the Lord by their beliefs). Interestingly, the Lord hated both the deeds and the doctrines of the Nicolaitans, which suggests that they justified their deeds by a set of doctrines.

Both of these groups therefore sought to justify their actions by claiming it was acceptable to do as they pleased, perhaps using scripture, or some other form of 'spiritual' credibility, to back up their claims. The problem, it seemed, particularly in this area of Asia, was the tendency to mix and match religious belief, in much the same way as we now see moves to combine 'faiths' rather than have a particular faith – i.e. Christianity (which always seems to be the faith that has to compromise most to achieve this!) This is achieved by trawling through scriptures, finding isolated texts suggesting unity with other beliefs, and then claiming that we all believe in the same God. Once such a compromise is reached, the erosion begins, and we become weakened and ineffectual.

Pergamos is very near to Istanbul/Constantinople, which has a rich history of allowing such compromises (East meets West

57. Pergamum was also the famous site of the temple to Aesculapius, the Greek God of healing supposed to be the founder of medical science, immortalized in the sky as the constellation Ophiuchus. The city became the seat of Babylonian sun worship, a center of idolatry and demon-controlled religions with splendid temples to nature. People from all over the Roman Empire came to seek healing in this pagan temple and the shrine area was inhabited by thousands of harmless snakes. On the hills of Acropolis stood resplendent buildings, statuary, palaces and the great library as well as the temples and an altar of Zeus the Saviour. Medicine and science was worshipped here and the symbol of their worship was the serpent. The snake is still used today as a symbol of healing, a staff entwined with serpents called the caduceus, representing the medical arts; Aesculapius is depicted holding the caduceus in his hand.'

here), and I would suggest that the universal worship of the Beast will be made possible from [58]compromises reached between the world's major religions, Muslim, Roman Catholic, Christian, Sikh, etc., who will all point to the Beast's, or False Prophet's, miracles and power as proof of his deity. Clearly this Church at Pergamos was beginning to entertain such thoughts of compromise, through allowing the Balaam and Nicolaitan followers to exist within their ranks, and was therefore brought into line by the Lord. Again repentance is called for and the Spirit expects an overcoming in their particular situation.

This time the reward is the *'hidden manna'* and as the only manna to survive was that collected and stored in the [59]Ark of the covenant, this may give some meaning to what was happening to the faithful at Pergamos regarding provision for their daily bread (and may also refer to the reappearance of the [60]Ark itself in the thousand year reign). The future is bleak for those who later refuse the mark of the Beast, as they cannot [61]buy or sell without his mark, and perhaps this was the situation in Pergamos for believers at that time, being pressured into submission to Emperor worship in order to access public welfare, which might include their daily provision, or manna. The white stone seems to have had two purposes. The first was as a ticket to access public events, and the other was as a voting tool, to determine whether an accused person was guilty (black stone) or innocent (white stone.) The person tried was handed one or the other stones, to represent the verdict. Both the manna, and the new name are hidden, and so this may be the

---

58. Istanbul is held as the seat of the 12th Imam, the expected Muslim 'messiah' by some of the 'twelvers' as they are called.

59. Hebrews 9:4.

60. The ark was not listed in the spoils of the Babylonian occupation of Jerusalem, its whereabouts being the subject of much conjecture, and believed by some to be buried in the catacombs below Jerusalem. Rev 11:19 may explain where it actually went.

61. Revelation 13:17.

Lord's way of telling them that their faithfulness is hidden with Him, but their vindication in being handed the white stone, will be eternal, and public!

Thyatira

Revelation 2:18- 29: *And unto the angel of the church in Thyatira write; These things saith the Son of God, Who hath His eyes like unto a flame of fire, and His feet are like fine brass; I know thy works, and charity, and service, and faith, and thy patience, and thy works; and the last to be more than the first. Notwithstanding I have a few things against thee, because thou sufferest that woman Jezebel, which calleth herself a prophetess, to teach and to seduce My servants to commit fornication, and to eat things sacrificed unto idols. And I gave her space to repent of her fornication; and she repented not. Behold, I will cast her into a bed, and them that commit adultery with her into great tribulation, except they repent of their deeds. And I will kill her children with death; and all the churches shall know that I am He which searcheth the reins and hearts: and I will give unto every one of you according to your works. But unto you I say, and unto the rest in Thyatira, as many as have not this doctrine, and which have not known the depths of Satan, as they speak; I will put upon you none other burden. But that which ye have already hold fast till I come. And he that overcometh, and keepeth My works unto the end, to him will I give power over the nations: And he shall rule them with a rod of iron; as the vessels of a potter shall they be broken to shivers: even as I received of My Father. And I will give him the morning star. He that hath an ear, let him hear what the Spirit saith unto the churches.*

The message is to the minister, in the first instance, who the Lord confirms is right in His sight, his zeal for the things of God being increased as he goes along. Nevertheless, this man is called to task because he permits the woman named as Jezebel to teach as a prophetess, promoting fornication and the involvement in idol worship. The Lord's judgement for her, her followers and her children is for them to be cast into 'great tribulation', and it seems that time has almost run out. For her, this probably meant she would be killed in the later persecutions, which were to follow for these people (but the message for the latter-day Jews following such false prophets with similar teachings equates to the events of the last three and a half years of the last week). Her judgement would come in such a way that all the churches would recognise the Lord's hand in it, as He that searches the 'reins and hearts' (= lit, kidneys and hearts, the unseen inner organs) so that while her fornication and idolatry might have looked to some to be justified by the doctrines she produced to back it up, it would be the actual deeds that would be judged and condemned by the Lord. The Lord doesn't seem to require anything more of this man other than to deliver the message to the Church, and to deal finally with this woman.

There were no more burdens for them except to continue in faithfulness, and overcome. Again it is the doctrine they held which determined their place, and while the minister obviously does not agree with her doctrines or deeds, he has not previously been strong enough to stop her. Again, this town was effectively run by the trade guilds, these being associated with the local worship of Zeus, father of the gods, and Apollos, his son. At this time Domitian was claiming to be Apollos and therefore the son of God. We can see that for any believer, association with a man claiming to be the son of God was dangerous spiritually. This would necessarily mean rejection for those skilled traders who did not partake of the trade guild feasts where business was conducted. Drinking, feasting and orgies were the order of the day here, and it is most likely that Jezebel had found some sort of 'compromise' that would allow believers who followed her teachings, to partake of the feasts, whilst deceiving themselves it was acceptable with God. They were bringing judgement down on themselves through their involvement with that present world.

When the over-comers rule with the Lord there will be no such indecision, for they will rule with the [62]rod of iron, and any nations who fail to submit will be broken to pieces, under the Lord's rule. The Lord makes reference to the morning star here, and we see this also mentioned in Rev 22:16, where He takes this title to Himself. In view of what is said to this Church I suggest this means that in the Lord's kingdom, such light will be given so as not to allow men to be deceived by false prophets such as this Jezebel. Remember that those described here have known the depths of Satan, and so their methods would not be that obvious, until the Lord, or the Holy Spirit, gave an insight into them.

Sardis

Revelation 3:1-6: *And unto the angel of the church in Sardis write; These things saith He that hath the seven Spirits of God, and the seven stars; I know thy works, that thou hast a name that thou livest, and art dead. Be watchful, and strengthen the things which remain, that are ready to die: for I have not found thy works perfect before God. Remember therefore how thou hast received and heard, and hold fast, and repent. If therefore thou shalt not watch, I will come on thee as a thief, and thou shalt not know what hour I will come upon thee. Thou hast a few names even in Sardis which have not defiled their garments;*

62. Said to be an iron-tipped staff that the potter uses to break items that do not come up to standard

and they shall walk with Me in white: for they are worthy. He that overcometh, the same shall be clothed in white raiment; and I will not blot out his name out of the book of life, but I will confess his name before My Father, and before His angels. He that hath an ear, let him hear what the Spirit saith unto the churches.

No compromise here; the Lord referred to their works, but made no comment about them, as they did not impress Him. They trade on their reputation only, having once been right, but now in decline, so that even that which they had is under threat. Their works needed to be perfect in His sight for them to have been accepted, and from what is said to the other churches, this must relate to what doctrines they held, and what they have done with them. It is how they have 'received and heard' that should have been the foundation of their works. They are to stop the leaks, and be watchful. It would do no harm to consider the history of Sardis, for it has a bearing on what the Lord said to them, and identifies Him as the all-knowing one, having control both on earth, and in heaven.

Sardis came to prominence during the time of King Croesus, when it was the capital of an area called [63]Lydia. Sardis itself was near to a river rich in alluvial gold that could easily be taken out of the sand, and this made Sardis extremely wealthy. It was also considered an impregnable fortress, having sheer cliffs on three sides and strong defences on the fourth. King Croesus, having consulted the oracle of Delphi, waged war on the Persians, who were growing ever stronger under Cyrus. Being almost defeated in battle, Croesus withdrew into Sardis, trusting in its defences to keep him safe, and there awaited help from his allies. When Cyrus arrived, having viewed the fortifications, it

63. Roughly encompassing the area where the seven churches were.

was observed that there were few guards on one side of the cliff ramparts, as they were considered unnecessary. Reputedly, a soldier from the city, having dropped his helmet, was seen retrieving it when he climbed down the cliff face. Cyrus, hearing about this, gave instructions for his soldiers to climb the cliff at night, and was then able to overcome Sardis.

Where they considered themselves strongest, they were vulnerable, and in their arrogance they failed to keep watch. The Lord's words therefore, that He would come on them as a thief (as He also spoke in the Gospels) should have rung alarm bells with this Church.

This also shows that the faithful Jews of this time did not have to be unaware of the 'times and seasons' and that providing they were watchful, as the Lord told them to be, He would not come on them as a thief. A reputation for righteousness or strength is not enough, in the Lord's view, and these had become complacent. Because their earlier efforts produced results, they stopped putting the effort in, and the blessing diminished to the extent that the majority were in real danger of failure. The responsibility was placed on their minister, whose real status here was 'dead'. It is only a few that have stayed faithful, and for them (and any that took note of this message) there was blessing. It seemed that what they started out with was good, and the Lord exhorted them to return to it, and then to hold on to it. This is where they had failed. There was no opposition mentioned to this church, because they are 'dead', and therefore had nothing to oppose.

Sadly the only opposition here would come to the faithful, in having to overcome the complacency of their fellow Church members in order to maintain their own enthusiasm. This is hard to do if all around you are negative or dismissive of the impending disaster. For the latter-day Jewish believer complacency is not an option; it will lead to his being swallowed up in the great tribulation, and almost certain death. If the Jews do not get the message, but trust to their own strength as this Church did, and refuse to listen to the Lord's advice to get out, then they will probably be among the many killed in Israel. It has to have got bad in this Church for the Lord to threaten to remove their names out of the book of life, for in effect this means eternal judgement for them, through their not being watchful.

Philadelphia

Revelation 3: 7-13: *And to the angel of the church in Philadelphia write; These things saith He that is holy, He that is true, He that hath the key of David, He that openeth, and no man shutteth; and shutteth, and no man openeth; I know thy works: behold, I have set before thee an open door, and no man can shut it: for thou hast a little strength, and hast kept My Word, and hast not denied My name. Behold, I will make them of the synagogue of Satan, which say they are Jews, and are not, but do lie; behold, I will make them to come and worship before thy feet, and to know that I have loved thee. Because thou hast kept the Word of My patience, I also will keep thee from the hour of temptation, which shall come upon all the world, to try them that dwell upon the earth. Behold, I come quickly: hold that fast which thou hast, that no man take thy crown. Him that overcometh will I make a pillar in the temple of My God, and he shall go no more out: and I will write upon him the name of My God, and the name of the city of My God, which is new Jerusalem, which cometh down out of heaven from My God: and I will write upon him My new name. He that hath an ear, let him hear what the Spirit saith unto the churches.*

The Lord's reference to the key of David shows that He has the power both to open and to close, and for those at Philadelphia, the door was opened. To the Jew this was an obvious reference to Isaiah 22:15, where the key of David was spoken of in the context of Shebna, the treasurer, losing his place to [64]Eliakim. The treasurer would have made decisions concerning the house of David, and been a trusted servant. In the verses we are considering the Lord talked of Himself as having this key, and in Rev 1:18 He says "I am He that liveth and was dead, and behold I am alive for evermore. Amen, and have the keys of hell and death", and so it is, that the Lord, having overcome death, now has control over it. However, when He spoke to the Philadelphians, it is in a different context, and has to do with having control over the future of the nation Israel, personified in David. To these people, He presents the positive aspect of His control, in that He is not only able to open the doors of the coming kingdom but is also able to determine the outcome for them. The key-holder is the one with the practical authority, who can be depended upon to make the right decisions.

Philadelphia has the same problem as the believers in Smyrna, where the danger came from within; those who had an outward profession of belief, but in reality pursued their own agenda. The Philadelphians were under pressure to deny the Lord's name, and the synagogue of Satan probably referred to those of them that had found a compromise within the society, thus allowing worship in both camps. The Lord made little of the opposition that the true believers faced here, but their ultimate reward reflects their status, and was equal to their faith.

64. It should be noted that both Eliakim, and Peter, who was also given the keys, were subject to fleshly weakness; Peter, not long after this, contradicted the Lord. Isaiah 22:25, and Mat 16:22. Only the Lord can do this properly, although He does uphold his servants.

My guess is that the faithful Philadelphians made little of the opposition either; they just put up with it, accepting it cheerfully in the right spirit. My impression from the Lord's words to them is that the Philadelphian believers were not highly regarded there, and had no say in what went on. Probably the Jews of the synagogue of Satan were more highly respected in this society, and were the ones 'holding the keys', or influencing all the decisions. These would be made eventually, to recognise just who the faithful were! We cannot be sure of the fate of the early church at Philadelphia, and it is by no means certain that they lived long lives. The promise from the Lord was His ability to keep them safe spiritually, as a mark of His respect for their holding fast. They were promised that they would be pillars in the (new) temple of God, a place far better than that of any other building on earth. They also will *go no more out,* as they may have also suffered in their lives. To be a 'pillar of society' in [65]God's new temple means that they are trusted, an example to others, like a key holder.

The other promise is in regard to the 'New Jerusalem', the one to come from heaven, and they are to be given the new name of God, the title of ownership, which contrasts with the mark of the Beast, the ownership of Satan (in its final application) from which they are protected. This shows that having a little strength, keeping His Word and not denying His name is all that the Lord requires in His latter-day Jewish believers, who are quite probably to be despised and shut out of normal society through their refusal to compromise. He makes the point that the hour of temptation comes on all the earth, and there will be no escape in these times; decisions will have

---

65. As there is no temple in the New Jerusalem, this probably refers to the millenium reign, and that later they will be accepted into the new Heaven and new Earth.

to made that may cost men their lives. There is no guarantee that believers will live or escape death in the last times, but their resurrection and reward is sure, providing that they hold fast. The point here is that it is the Lord Who has the final authority on whether one is strengthened to hold fast, or not, for the decision on who makes it into the real kingdom is ultimately His! Lastly, this church is aptly named as Philadelphia, or love of the brethren, for whatever their persecutions, they managed to stick together, to see it through!

Laodicea

Revelation 3:14-22: *And unto the angel of the church of the Laodiceans write; These things saith the Amen, the faithful and true witness, the beginning of the creation of God; I know thy works, that thou art neither cold nor hot: I would thou wert cold or hot. So then because thou art lukewarm, and neither cold nor hot, I will spue thee out of My mouth. Because thou sayest, I am rich, and increased with goods, and have need of nothing; and knowest not that thou art wretched, and miserable, and poor, and blind, and naked: I counsel thee to buy of Me gold tried in the fire, that thou mayest be rich; and white raiment, that thou mayest be clothed, and that the shame of thy nakedness do not appear; and anoint thine eyes with eyesalve, that thou mayest see. As many as I love, I rebuke and chasten: be zealous therefore, and repent. Behold, I stand at the door, and knock: if any man hear My voice, and open the door, I will come in to him, and will sup with him, and He with Me. To him that overcometh will I grant to sit with Me in My throne, even as I also overcame, and am set down with My Father in His throne. He that hath an ear, let him hear what the Spirit saith unto the churches.*

If we accept that the Lord is writing initially to the angel, or minister of the church, it is a fair assumption that the members of the church would follow his example. Here however the message is that because of the lukewarm nature of the leader(s), they will be spewed out of the Lord's mouth, unless they change. The Lord establishes that His is the 'true witness' and that He as the 'chief over God's creation' is speaking to a people that do not know the true state of affairs; they are not aware of their true status in His sight. The Lord uses terminology that they will understand, and is urging them to trust Him.

Laodicea was situated in the middle of several important trade routes, making it a centre of distribution, and consequently extremely wealthy. Its weakness was that it did not have an independent water supply, and relied upon a system of aqueducts to bring water from hot springs situated about five miles distant. In contrast to Hierapolis with its medicinal hot springs, or Colossae with its supply of cold water, Laodicea had to fetch its water through stone pipes from hot springs at Denizli some five miles away, and by the time it reached Laodicea the water was lukewarm.

Hierapolis, Colossae and Laodicea are situated close together, and are associated together in Paul's [66]writings, so we can see that the Lord's comparison here with water would be a graphic illustration of how their works (not themselves, necessarily) would be distasteful, or insipid to the Lord, neither refreshing, or medicinal – of no real use. We have only to look to the Philadelphians to see what was acceptable to the Lord in terms of works, where essentially they were reliant on the Lord, having had *a little strength, thou hast kept My Word, and hast not denied My name.* In direct contrast, the Laodiceans were

66. Colossians 4:12-16.

extremely well off and self-sufficient, and failed to see their need of [67]help in any form. This would seem to be the main problem, that their eyes needed opening to the true situation, having been blinded by their abundance. The real state of things, pitiable, poor, blind and naked, is set against their own estimation of themselves. They needed *gold, tried in the fire* (ie faith, the real riches without the impurities) white raiment (Laodicea was famed for its black wool products) and eyesalve (The Lord spat on the ground, John 9: 6-11) to make this, and sent the man to wash in the pool of Siloam. Laodicea reputedly produced its own medicinal product, called Phrygian powder, a sort of pumice mixed with oil, expensive but probably of no real use). The point really being that in everything you could point to, the Laodiceans seemed to have it available, so where was the need for the Lord?

This is a rebuke and chastening, and yet the Lord here advised them, rather than commanded them. They were to be zealous or hot, perhaps as the healing springs nearby, going back to the source, and to repent, or simply to turn around. The Lord here is knocking on the door that they have put in the way. This had nothing to do with the opening of the door that He has the key to, the barriers here were theirs, and the onus was on them to allow the Lord to be heard. The sad thing here is that they were believers, not unbelievers, as this passage is often said to portray. The Lord was not asking them to open their hearts to believe on Him, as sinners. He was actually trying to get through to people who had previously accepted Him, but because of their own self-satisfaction, were too complacent to even hear His Word. Why should they need Him now? They considered that they were doing fine without Him!

67. When the city was demolished by an earthquake in 60AD, it was rebuilt completely from its own wealth, no application being made to the Roman authorities for help!.

This attitude is reminiscent of the Lord's warning concerning the days of Noah:

Luke 17:26-36: *And as it was in the days of Noe, so shall it be also in the days of the Son of Man. They did eat, they drank, they married wives, they were given in marriage, until the day that Noe entered into the ark, and the flood came, and destroyed them all. Likewise also as it was in the days of Lot; they did eat, they drank, they bought, they sold, they planted, they builded; But the same day that Lot went out of Sodom it rained fire and brimstone from heaven, and destroyed them all. Even thus shall it be in the day when the Son of Man is revealed. In that day, he which shall be upon the housetop, and his stuff in the house, let him not come down to take it away: and he that is in the field, let him likewise not return back. Remember Lot's wife. Whosoever shall seek to save his life shall lose it; and whosoever shall lose his life shall preserve it. I tell you, in that night there shall be two men in one bed; the one shall be taken, and the other shall be left. Two women shall be grinding together; the one shall be taken, and the other left. Two men shall be in the field; the one shall be taken, and the other left.*

The sad thing is that in their contentment to eat and drink in these times, they will miss out on the opportunity to eat and drink with the Lord. This could be argued to mean that to eat and drink with Him involves our communion, sharing in His experiences both of suffering and resurrection, so showing the Lord's death till He comes. Ultimately those that share in earthly suffering for Him will also partake of His heavenly blessing, and it is this heavenly place that the Laodiceans are in danger of missing.

Will the latter-day Jews be prepared to leave what they have to flee into the mountains when the time comes? This is the question here.

CHAPTER NINE

SEVEN SEALS

✿

Having looked at the seven churches, our attention is now drawn to the heavenly aspect, where John is called up to see things from a new vantage point.

The remainder of the Book of Revelation is divided up between the 'seven seals', referring to the opening of the 'book' or scroll, held by God. The first six seals would seem to cover the whole period of the seven last years of the last week, with the last seal giving their completion. Whilst John is shown what is about take place overall, I would suggest that these seals represent an overview, given before the real events occur. Once the seventh seal is opened, we return to the beginning again, to the first trumpet.

The seven trumpets start off these events, containing the wrath of the Lamb and the [68]seven thunders, but they do not seem to follow each other in any regularly spaced sequence; rather the first six events are announced almost simultaneously, the exception being the sounding of the seventh trumpet, which ushers in the final period of three and a half years.

Finally the 'last seven plagues, or the seven vials' containing the wrath of God, follow on from the sounding of the last trumpet, and include both the destruction of Babylon and the armies of the Beast, which then takes us to the conclusion of the final week.

68. Which although John heard, he was directed not to write them down.

Although there are similarities between these events, difficulties appear if we try and link them directly to one another. They should be considered separately, as they apply to different times. There is an exception, however, for the seven seals correspond perfectly with the Lord's words regarding the last week of the seventy weeks, and these two should be considered together.

The Seven Seals: Revelation 4:1–8:6

Revelation 4:1-11: *After this I looked, and, behold, a door was opened in heaven: and the first voice which I heard was as it were of a trumpet talking with me; which said, Come up hither, and I will shew thee things which must be hereafter. And immediately I was in the spirit: and, behold, a throne was set in heaven, and one sat on the throne. And He that sat was to look upon like a jasper and a sardine stone: and there was a rainbow round about the throne, in sight like unto an emerald. And round about the throne were four and twenty seats: and upon the seats I saw four and twenty elders sitting, clothed in white raiment; and they had on their heads crowns of gold. And out of the throne proceeded lightnings and thunderings and voices: and there were seven lamps of fire burning before the throne, which are the seven Spirits of God. And before the throne there was a sea of glass like unto crystal: and in the midst of the throne, and round about the throne, were four beasts full of eyes before and behind. And the first beast was like a lion, and the second beast like a calf, and the third beast had a face as a man, and the fourth beast was like a flying eagle. And the four beasts had each of them six wings about him; and they were full of eyes within: and they rest not day and night, saying, Holy, holy, holy, Lord God Almighty, which was, and is, and is to come. And when those beasts give glory and honour and thanks to Him that sat on the throne, Who liveth for ever and ever,*

The four and twenty elders fall down before Him that sat on the throne, and worship Him that liveth for ever and ever, and cast their crowns before the throne, saying, Thou art worthy, O Lord, to receive glory and honour and power: for Thou hast created all things, and for Thy pleasure they are and were created.

John, in his own words is now 'in the spirit', and transported to heaven, where he is to be shown 'things which must be hereafter.' This establishes that what he had previously seen regarding the churches was on earth, and concerned that present time. There is therefore no need to look for a fulfilment of a group of seven Asian churches in any [69]future time, although the lessons contained within these earlier chapters must surely illustrate to a future body of Jewish believers, the pitfalls and dangers they might face. There are various assertions concerning these churches, for example as representing the various ages of the Gentile churches, even to giving the different 'ages' a date, along with similar interpretations of what they mean. The fact is that these were groups of Jewish believers who were present in John's time, with specific needs and problems, and to whom the Lord wrote through John. There is no evidence or hint in scripture that they will be found in later times, nor that they in some way represent a future Gentile church, in all its throes of development, however appealing these theories are to the ear. Sorry, but there it is!

What John sees now is the throne of God, and God Himself described as a jasper and sardine stone, or taking both together a 'translucent red' with a rainbow of emerald green around Him. As well as His appearance, we are told that lightnings, thunderings and voices come from the throne, and therefore

69. The seven churches play no further part in the narrative, and are not mentioned again!

from God Himself. Also there are twenty-four elders about the throne, and seven lamps of fire (not the seven churches associated with them, but the spirits of God themselves.) In addition, also round about the throne, are the four cherubim, associated with creation, as the four creatures with dominion over the earth. These are described as being 'full of eyes' and these may well be the 'watchers' that appear in [70]Daniel, who judge Nebuchadnezzar with such authority. They are given the power to instigate praise in the heavens, with the elders following their lead. Interestingly Satan once held a similar position, for he is described as the "anointed cherub that [71]covereth", but in the tabernacle, as here, there are two cherubim that cover the mercy-seat, and two embroidered on the veil, making four altogether, each having the characteristics of the others. No longer is such power given to one being, as these four seem to have to agree together, before they can act.

Revelation 5:1-5: *And I saw in the right hand of Him that sat on the throne a book written within and on the backside, sealed with seven seals. And I saw a strong angel proclaiming with a loud voice, Who is worthy to open the book, and to loose the seals thereof? And no man in heaven, nor in earth, neither under the earth, was able to open the book, neither to look thereon. And I wept much, because no man was found worthy to open and to read the book, neither to look thereon. And one of the elders saith unto me, Weep not: behold, the Lion of the tribe of Juda, the Root of David, hath prevailed to open the book, and to loose the seven seals thereof.*

---

70. Of course, the seven spirits may also fit this description, as the 'eyes of the Lord' Revelation 5:6.

71. Ezekiel 28:14, worth reading the whole of this description. Compare also Chapter 1, for another description of the cherubim and the throne.

The beginning of the unfolding of the purposes of God in His creation is written in the book. Interestingly, it needs to be opened by a man, as there is a search made for someone worthy to do this, and no one is found, not presently living, or dead, or indeed in heaven! This would include the 24 elders, who have been redeemed from the earth.

Revelation 5:6-14: *And I beheld, and, lo, in the midst of the throne and of the four beasts, and in the midst of the elders, stood a Lamb as it had been slain, having seven horns and seven eyes, which are the seven Spirits of God sent forth into all the earth. And He came and took the book out of the right hand of Him that sat upon the throne. And when He had taken the book, the four beasts and four and twenty elders fell down before the Lamb, having every one of them harps, and golden vials full of odours, which are the prayers of saints. And they sung a new song, saying, Thou art worthy to take the book, and to open the seals thereof: for Thou wast slain, and hast redeemed us to God by Thy blood out of every kindred, and tongue, and people, and nation; And hast made us unto our God kings and priests: and we shall reign on the earth. And I beheld, and I heard the voice of many angels round about the throne and the beasts and the elders: and the number of them was ten thousand times ten thousand, and thousands of thousands; Saying with a loud voice, Worthy is the Lamb that was slain to receive power, and riches, and wisdom, and strength, and honour, and glory, and blessing. And every creature which is in heaven, and on the earth, and under the earth, and such as are in the sea, and all that are in them, heard I saying, Blessing, and honour, and glory, and power, be unto Him that sitteth upon the throne, and unto the Lamb for ever and ever. And the four beasts said, Amen. And the four and twenty elders fell down and worshipped Him that liveth for ever and ever.*

The one who is found worthy is the Lord, Who in His title of the 'Lion of the tribe of Judah, the root of David' is the man who is sought. It is in His title of the 'Lamb as it had been slain' that He claims the right to open the book, and the four beasts and the elders join in singing His praises. This is not only the book of the judgement of the earth, but the hope of the living and the dead in Him. Note that the elders hold the vials, full of the prayers of saints, which implies they are representative of the rest who are awaiting their own redemption. After this is the description of the opening of the seals. If we remember that these events are revealed as the book is opened, as if we are being given a taste of what each chapter contains, we can understand that it is not until the book is fully opened that the events begin, being individually heralded by the trumpets. This will help us when we try to compare the seals with the trumpets, for although they are concurrent in places; they do not match exactly.

First seal

Revelation 6:1-2: *And I saw when the Lamb opened one of the seals, and I heard, as it were the noise of thunder, one of the four beasts saying, Come and see. And I saw, and behold a white horse: and he that sat on him had a bow; and a crown was given unto him: and he went forth conquering, and to conquer.*

Only in this first seal is the noise of thunder mentioned, perhaps a 'loud crack' as the seal is opened? This may be true for the other seals as well, but we are not told this. The four beasts or cherubim are involved with the first four seals, and this first one depicts a figure given a bow and a crown, and his mission is to overcome in the earth. This figure has been previously identified by some as the Lord, because of the white horse with which He is later associated, but if we remember what the Lord Himself taught consistently about the beginning of these events…

Matthew 24:4-5: *And Jesus answered and said unto them, Take heed that no man deceive you. For many shall come in My name, saying, I am Christ; and shall deceive many.*

…then we can see that this first figure is representative of the 'many that shall come in My name, saying I am Christ', an imposter with the intention of deceiving the faithful and unfaithful alike. This effort to deceive does not stop when the second seal is opened, but continues throughout the time. We must view each of these seals as progressively adding to the previous troubles.

Second seal

Revelation 6:3-4: *And when He had opened the second seal, I heard the second beast say, Come and see. And there went out another horse that was red: and power was given to him that sat thereon to take peace from the earth, and that they should kill one another: and there was given unto him a great sword.*

Again, one of the cherubim calls John to view events, and here he sees a red horse, the rider having the power to take peace from the [72]earth. This should not move the faithful believer however, for he should not be troubled, providing he knows that

---

72. As wars are nothing new, this must relate to a spiritual condition, a change in dispensation toward men. Consider Luke 2:14, and then compare Matthew 10:34. This marks the end of the period of Grace offered in the Lord's coming to earth.

'All these things must come to pass'. This is where an understanding of events is critical, for knowing what is to occur beforehand shapes our later thinking and actions. The whole purpose of John being given this revelation to publish throughout the Church is to inform men of God's purpose, so they are not then surprised and terrified when it comes. Those that lightly esteem prophetic teaching are the ones most likely to be caught unawares when it turns out that there is no peaceful solution for the world through men's efforts. The best minds available are now seeking resolutions for the problems of the Middle East, and every attempt comes to nothing – it just gets worse!

Matthew 24:6-7: *And ye shall hear of wars and rumours of wars: see that ye be not troubled: for all these things must come to pass, but the end is not yet. For nation shall rise against nation, and kingdom against kingdom.*

Third seal

Revelation 6:5-6: *And when He had opened the third seal, I heard the third beast say, Come and see. And I beheld, and lo a black horse; and he that sat on him had a pair of balances in his hand. And I heard a voice in the midst of the four beasts say, A measure of wheat for a penny, and three measures of barley for a penny; and see thou hurt not the oil and the wine.*

Again John is given an invitation to view events, as the third seal is broken. This time it is a rider on a black horse, and he has a pair of balances. This would indicate trade, and he is given authority to determine the economic balance of the earth, in a detrimental sense, for he is told not to hurt or interfere with the oil and the wine. We are not told what this means, but a comparison with the story of the [73]Samaritan who pours in oil and wine as a healing compound for wounds inflicted by the robbers may indicate that medical treatment will not be affected, or that possibly those that show compassion in this age may also be shown compassion themselves, and these things will not affect them. From the Lord's description of future famine, pestilence and earthquakes, it is easy to see how the world's great economies will be stretched to their limits, trying to provide aid to so many in need. Famine and disease inevitably follow wars, but earthquakes are less predictable, and fault lines run through most countries. Once the earth starts its '[74]groaning' it will continue until the Lord rules, and sets things right. Compare what the Lord said:

Matthew 24:7-8: ...*and there shall be famines, and pestilences, and earthquakes, in divers places. All these are the beginning of sorrows.*

Fourth seal

Revelation 6:7-8: *And when He had opened the fourth seal, I heard the voice of the fourth beast say, Come and see. And I looked, and behold a pale horse: and his name that sat on him was Death, and Hell followed with him. And power was given unto them over the fourth part of the earth, to kill with sword, and with hunger, and with death, and with the beasts of the earth.*

This is the last seal that John is invited to see by the beast, or cherubim, and it again concerns the earth. We are told that the

---

73. Luke 10.34.
74. Compare Romans 8:19-23, for the time draws closer for our own redemption, after which the world will become settled.

rider is restricted to the 'fourth part of the earth' and from the word for earth (= region) I would suggest that this is more local to Israel, namely the Middle East, so that the main thrust of these disasters centres around Israel and its neighbours. When we compare what the Lord said this would seem consistent, for the hatred is from all nations, but for the most part the betrayal is from within, no doubt stirred up by the false prophets arising at the same time that the Gospel of the Kingdom is being preached by the faithful Jews. Clearly this ministry is savagely opposed, because in essence it points to the Jews becoming the dominant people of the earth, under God's hand. This news is bound to upset the Muslim world, who themselves seek after prominence under their own 'messiah' and probably will upset some Roman Catholics, Christians, Sikhs, etc. to some extent as well. It is certain to provoke unfavourable consequences for Israel. The exhortation is now for the people to endure and remain faithful, regardless of what their end involves.

Matthew 24:9-14: *Then shall they deliver you up to be afflicted, and shall kill you: and ye shall be hated of all nations for My name's sake. And then shall many be offended, and shall betray one another, and shall hate one another. And many false prophets shall rise, and shall deceive many. And because iniquity shall abound, the love of many shall wax cold. But he that shall endure unto the end, the same shall be saved. And this gospel of the kingdom shall be preached in all the world for a witness unto all nations; and then shall the end come.*

From these words, I suggest that the first 'end' that the Lord is talking about is the end of the persecution, which for some will mean being faithful up to their own demise. Some of the faithful will not make alive it to the end, but this will not affect their salvation in any way. The second 'end', coming after the gospel of the Kingdom is preached must refer to the period of the second half of the week, the 'great tribulation'. However, the events described in these verses above and within the fourth seal are what we have learned to call the beginnings of sorrows, which lead up to the setting up of the Beast over Israel. Clearly, the first half of the week involves major persecution for the Jew wherever he may be, but when compared to the very 'end' the time of the Beast's rule for three and a half years, these things are but a foretaste of what is to come.

Fifth seal

Revelation 6:9-11: *And when He had opened the fifth seal, I saw under the altar the souls of them that were slain for the Word of God, and for the testimony which they held: And they cried with a loud voice, saying, How long, O Lord, holy and true, dost Thou not judge and avenge our blood on them that dwell on the earth? And white robes were given unto every one of them; and it was said unto them, that they should rest yet for a little season, until their fellowservants also and their brethren, that should be killed as they were, should be fulfilled.*

Events now transfer to heaven, and from there John could clearly see what had taken place, without having to be invited. Interestingly, those slain for their testimony who had refused to compromise or let go, those who had endured to their end, are held 'under the altar', their sacrifice having been accepted. Their cry is for vengeance on them that 'dwell on the earth', and whilst we know that these things are allowed in the will of God, and that they are spiritually inspired, it is by the hand of man that the atrocities have been committed. We see that they are told to be at rest, for the retribution of God has not yet taken place. There are yet more to be killed when the Beast starts on his real mission to establish himself above all, being the representative of Satan's power on the earth.

Matthew 24:15-28: *When ye therefore shall see the abomination of desolation, spoken of by Daniel the prophet, stand in the holy place, (whoso readeth, let him understand:) Then let them which be in Judaea flee into the mountains: Let him which is on the housetop not come down to take any thing out of his house: Neither let him which is in the field return back to take his clothes. And woe unto them that are with child, and to them that give suck in those days! But pray ye that your flight be not in the winter, neither on the sabbath day: For then shall be great tribulation, such as was not since the beginning of the world to this time, no, nor ever shall be. And except those days should be shortened, there should no flesh be saved: but for the elect's sake those days shall be shortened. Then if any man shall say unto you, Lo, here is Christ, or there; believe it not. For there shall arise false Christs, and false prophets, and shall shew great signs and wonders; insomuch that, if it were possible, they shall deceive the very elect. Behold, I have told you before. Wherefore if they shall say unto you, Behold, He is in the desert; go not forth: behold, He is in the secret chambers; believe it not. For as the lightning cometh out of the east, and shineth even unto the west; so shall also the coming of the Son of Man be. For wheresoever the carcase is, there will the eagles be gathered together.*

The Lord's strong advice in these times is not for men to wait and be killed but to escape the persecutions by flight, as previously discussed, through Jordan. This is now the period of the great tribulation, the latter half of the week, where the Beast starts to exalt himself as a spiritual being, above God Himself.

The Jews' worship has been stopped, and they are not to look for any deliverance on earth; rather they should hide in the place appointed for them, and wait for the Lord's sign to appear in the heavens, for their deliverance. These are frightening times, and any caught are likely to have to face the image of the Beast, and all that will involve.

Sixth seal

Revelation 6:12-17: *And I beheld when He had opened the sixth seal, and, lo, there was a great earthquake; and the sun became black as sackcloth of hair, and the moon became as blood; And the stars of heaven fell unto the earth, even as a fig tree casteth her untimely figs, when she is shaken of a mighty wind. And the heaven departed as a scroll when it is rolled together; and every mountain and island were moved out of their places. And the kings of the earth, and the great men, and the rich men, and the chief captains, and the mighty men, and every bondman, and every free man, hid themselves in the dens and in the rocks of the mountains; And said to the mountains and rocks, Fall on us, and hide us from the face of Him that sitteth on the throne, and from the wrath of the Lamb: For the great day of His wrath is come; and who shall be able to stand?*

The sixth seal covers the period of the last half of the week, but we should remember that the timing of these seals cannot be pinned down exactly, as we are looking at the opening of the book as a whole, rather than a chronological series of events. Therefore this seal mainly describes the end of the last seven years, but can also include events within the 'end' period itself. In comparison with later scriptures, we will learn that, for example, Satan and his angels will be cast out into the earth, and that this will have an effect on the intensity of the persecution toward Israel. The stars of heaven falling could indicate these momentous heavenly events taking place, and the further earthquakes and volcanic activity associated here could cause the darkening of the sun and moon over a long period.

What is suggested here are worldwide disasters on a scale never before experienced, and this whole period is covered with both literal and spiritual darkness. It is in this gloomy setting that the world kingdom of the Beast is established, and finally ended. The introduction of the seven trumpets and of the seven vials will supply more detail of what is involved. When the sign of the Lord is revealed, after the tribulation, this is the time when the men that are left will realise that their hatred of the Jews and worship of the Beast have cost them dearly, and that what remains for them is the judgement of God for their rejection of the Gospel of the Kingdom that they had heard being preached, but rejected.

Matthew 24:29-30: *Immediately after the tribulation of those days shall the sun be darkened, and the moon shall not give her light, and the stars shall fall from heaven, and the powers of the heavens shall be shaken: And then shall appear the sign of the Son of Man in heaven: and then shall all the tribes of the earth mourn, and they shall see the Son of Man coming in the clouds of heaven with power and great glory.*

The Lord's words show the situation "immediately after the tribulation of those days", ie when the Beast has been overcome with his armies. But our attention is drawn to another activity that is clearly part of the sixth seal, and demonstrates that the writings and events that John describes are not always consecutive, but can be concurrent:

Revelation 7:1-3: *And after these things I saw four angels standing on the four corners of the earth, holding the four winds of the earth, that the wind should not blow on the earth, nor on the sea, nor on any tree. And I saw another angel ascending from the east, having the seal of the living God: and he cried with a loud voice to the four angels, to whom it was given to hurt the earth and the sea, Saying, Hurt not the earth, neither the sea, nor the trees, till we have sealed the servants of our God in their foreheads.*

The angel having the seal of the living God overrules the other angels, and another aspect of this last three and a half years of the great tribulation is revealed. The angels are shown withholding the winds. Imagine that as well as earthquakes and volcanic activity, the climate is also held in check. We can hardly imagine what this means for food production, and every aspect of normal life. These angels have power to hurt the earth, the sea and the trees, so that life will be a constant struggle during this time. But before this takes place, that is, at some point either during the first half of the week or the middle of it, there is a group of one hundred and forty-four thousand Jews selected to go through the tribulation period, untouched by it. If any can believe that these people are anything other than Jewish, they are truly misguided!

Revelation 7:4-8: *And I heard the number of them which were sealed: and there were sealed an hundred and forty and four thousand of all the tribes of the children of Israel. Of the tribe of Juda were sealed twelve thousand. Of the tribe of Reuben were sealed twelve thousand. Of the tribe of Gad were sealed twelve thousand. Of the tribe of Aser were sealed twelve thousand. Of the tribe of Nepthalim were sealed twelve thousand. Of the tribe of Manasses were sealed twelve thousand. Of the tribe of Simeon were sealed twelve thousand. Of the tribe of Levi were sealed twelve thousand. Of the tribe of Issachar were sealed twelve thousand. Of the tribe of Zabulon were sealed twelve thousand. Of the tribe of Joseph were sealed twelve thousand. Of the tribe of Benjamin were sealed twelve thousand.*

However, there is another group of people described who are before the throne, and therefore have previously died:

Revelation 7:9-17: *After this I beheld, and, lo, a great multitude, which no man could number, of all nations, and kindreds, and people, and tongues, stood before the throne, and before the Lamb, clothed with white robes, and palms in their hands; And cried with a loud voice, saying, Salvation to our God which sitteth upon the throne, and unto the Lamb. And all the angels stood round about the throne, and about the elders and the four beasts, and fell before the throne on their faces, and worshipped God, Saying, Amen: Blessing, and glory, and wisdom, and thanksgiving, and honour, and power, and might, be unto our God for ever and ever. Amen. And one of the elders answered, saying unto me, What are these which are arrayed in white robes? and whence came they? And I said unto him, Sir, thou knowest. And he said to me, These are they which came out of great tribulation, and have washed their robes, and made them white in the blood of the Lamb. Therefore are they before the throne of God, and serve Him day and night in His temple: and He that sitteth on the throne shall dwell among them. They shall hunger no more, neither thirst any more; neither shall the sun light on them, nor any heat. For the Lamb which is in the midst of the throne shall feed them, and shall lead them unto living fountains of waters: and God shall wipe away all tears from their eyes.*

It is revealed to John that this other group, who are not

necessarily Jewish, have also proved themselves righteous, and are worthy of the white robes they are given. They have suffered through hunger, thirst and exposure to the sun, which could indicate they have also become homeless or stateless, perhaps because of their support of the Jews, or their refusal to become subject to the Beast and his worship. These may be the adherents to the preaching of the kingdom that the two witnesses had ministered, prior to the middle of the week. In comparison, the Lord taught His disciples:

Matthew 24:31: *And He shall send His angels with a great sound of a trumpet, and they shall gather together His elect from the four winds, from one end of heaven to the other.*

It may be that this refers to the one hundred and forty-four thousand, who have a particular role in this second half of the week, but it is more likely that the Lord is referring to the Jews returning to their homeland after the tribulation is over and His kingdom is established under the auspices of the hundred and forty-four thousand, who [75]are the 'first-fruits' of the kingdom. I say this because it is unlikely that He will call His people back to undergo the sufferings of the tribulation after having warned them to flee from it.

Seventh seal

Revelation 8:1-6: *And when He had opened the seventh seal, there was silence in heaven about the space of half an hour. And I saw the seven angels which stood before God; and to them were given seven trumpets. And another angel came and stood at the altar, having a golden*

75. Revelation 14:4.

censer; and there was given unto him much incense, that he should offer it with the prayers of all saints upon the golden altar which was before the throne. And the smoke of the incense, which came with the prayers of the saints, ascended up before God out of the angel's hand. And the angel took the censer, and filled it with fire of the altar, and cast it into the earth: and there were voices, and thunderings, and lightnings, and an earthquake. And the seven angels which had the seven trumpets prepared themselves to sound.

The seventh seal, of course, is when the book is finally opened, and the events contained in it can commence. Its opening begins a short period of silence, and then John sees the seven angels with the seven trumpets prepared to sound, and unleash the events we have seen previewed in the opening of the seals. Before this, another angel offers incense mixed with the prayers of 'all saints', and once it had come to the attention of God Himself, the censer is filled with the fire of the altar and cast to the earth. What we see here is the end of the waiting period, and the prayers of the saints, along with the purpose of God, typified in the altar, and in His Son, are combined to commence the last week. Notice the seven trumpets are preceded by 'thunderings, lightnings and an earthquake' which mark the event, so it is reasonable to expect that this earthquake is a large one, and could be the [76]first event on earth to look for.

---

76. Compare this with Joel 2:30-31 to see that these types of natural disasters occur both at the beginning, during, and after the end of the 'Day of the Lord'; it is a "day of darkness, and of gloominess, a day of clouds and thick darkness" Joel 2:2.

THE SEVEN TRUMPETS, THE WRATH OF THE LAMB

❈

The first trumpet:

Revelation 8:7: *The first angel sounded, and there followed hail and fire mingled with blood, and they were cast upon the earth: and the third part of trees was burnt up, and all green grass was burnt up.*

The first four of these trumpets herald events to do with the earth, which could well be explained away by man as being produced by natural causes. However these are scriptural events described as the beginnings of the 'sorrows' brought upon the earth as the judgements of the Lamb. Most of us accept that these sorrows have been with us for a while, growing in intensity, building up to the final phase, but when we consider that these trumpets commence with the seals and book being fully opened, I would suggest that these disasters are unique to the seven-year period of the last week.

The earth, of course, is groaning as a sign of the times, but then it always has. Natural disasters have always been present, but these things are different, and it cannot be said for example, that 'hail and fire, mingled with blood' on this scale are common occurrences. Hail and fire were the third plague sent by God on

Egypt, and warning was given beforehand to any that would listen. When there is extreme volcanic activity, it is often accompanied by weather phenomena such 'St Elmo's fire', which is glowing points of fire on ships from the electrically-charged particles of rock and ash that are falling everywhere. This may be what is described here, or an extreme form of chain lightning. The plague in Egypt caused the [77]destruction of the trees and crops, with the aim of bringing the people to repentance, by their acknowledgment that "the earth is the Lord's". Here, of course, there is the addition of blood with the hail and fire, which would indicate the severity of the hail in causing bloodshed to man and animals, as well as severe damage to crops and trees.

The second trumpet

Revelation 8:8-9: *And the second angel sounded, and as it were a great mountain burning with fire was cast into the sea: and the third part of the sea became blood; And the third part of the creatures which were in the sea, and had life, died; and the third part of the ships were destroyed.*

Again, this could be considered a natural disaster and science tells us that tsunamis - freak giant waves - have occurred at various times throughout history. The tsunami is caused by volcanic activity or earthquakes which create widespread destruction, often many hundreds of miles away from where they have initially occurred. Freak waves are known to sink the biggest of ships, and are well known to mariners. Approximately one ship a week sinks, and some go down in mysterious

---

77. Exodus 9:23-26.

circumstances, often attributed to these waves, which are far beyond normal size, and against which ships have no defence. Again the trumpet signifies disaster on a scale never before known, affecting a third of the ships; so anything in its path is destroyed. There is a fault line off the coast of America and Canada which is expected to produce such a disaster in an area called the 'Cascadia fault' which would affect the whole Pacific area if the right conditions were met. There are of course many other fault lines in the world that could produce similar effects. The seas and rivers turning to blood are phenomena that have been seen before on a smaller scale, for example in 2001, when 'red rain' fell on parts of India for about two months. This turned out to be algae, and was thought to originate from dust entering the atmosphere from space.

The third trumpet

Revelation 8:10-11: *And the third angel sounded, and there fell a great star from heaven, burning as it were a lamp, and it fell upon the third part of the rivers, and upon the fountains of waters; And the name of the star is called Wormwood: and the third part of the waters became wormwood; and many men died of the waters, because they were made bitter.*

It is difficult to know what this star is, as angels themselves are described as stars in scripture, and it may well be this. However, from the description given, it is suggested we could be looking at a comet strike. Comets have been known to disintegrate in their latter stages and enter earth's atmosphere. They are relatively unpredictable, as they come from deep space, unlike asteroids, whose movements can be tracked well in advance. Their destructive power is immense, many times that of our largest nuclear bombs. When they strike, they send up a massive dust cloud, known as an airburst, and this can blot out the sun, causing light phenomena in the skies, as light is reflected from the cloud produced.

We cannot rule out the effects of nuclear fallout either, for this could be what John describes. The effect is that many men die from drinking the water, so the water does not seem to appear any different to normal, and the effects of this could be played down, to minimise panic. This does not necessarily refer to nuclear war, as it could also be the result of a nuclear test, a so-called 'dirty bomb'. Several nations are still keen to develop such bombs, if they do not already have them.

The fourth trumpet

Revelation 8:12: *And the fourth angel sounded, and the third part of the sun was smitten, and the third part of the moon, and the third part of the stars; so as the third part of them was darkened, and the day shone not for a third part of it, and the night likewise.*

Again the effects of the previous trumpets could cause this darkening of the sun, further affecting whole crop systems that are already weakened. We can see that these apparently natural disasters would begin to preoccupy the whole world, and countries such as America, and those in Europe which traditionally interfere to keep the 'status quo' in the Middle East would be hard pressed to send aid or exert influence over others, having their own internal problems to deal with. Politicians have to concern themselves with re-election, and ignoring the home front would be bad judgement for any government. This, of course, is apart from the fear, panic and frustrations that would prevail, and the opportunists will always be ready to riot, loot and pillage in such times.

The three woes

Revelation 8:1:3 *And I beheld, and heard an angel flying through the midst of heaven, saying with a loud voice, Woe, woe, woe, to the inhabiters of the earth by reason of the other voices of the trumpet of the three angels, which are yet to sound.*

After the first four trumpets we are now presented with the three woes, tied in with the last three trumpets that are to sound. These 'woes' (a basic expression of grief, or grievous events) are connected with the release of supernatural beings with the power to hurt and torment men, and are set in contrast with the previous trumpets that heralded what we might term natural disasters. As if things weren't bad enough, these now are released:

The fifth trumpet, the first woe:

Revelation 9:1-12: *And the fifth angel sounded, and I saw a star fall from heaven unto the earth: and to him was given the key of the bottomless pit. And he opened the bottomless pit; and there arose a smoke out of the pit, as the smoke of a great furnace; and the sun and the air were darkened by reason of the smoke of the pit. And there came out of the smoke locusts upon the earth: and unto them was given power, as the scorpions of the earth have power. And it was commanded them that they should not hurt the grass of the earth, neither any green thing, neither any tree; but only those men which have not the seal of God in their foreheads. And to them it was given that they should not kill them, but that they should be tormented five months: and their torment was as the torment of a scorpion, when he striketh a man. And in those days shall men seek death, and shall not find it; and shall desire to die, and death shall flee from them. And the shapes of the locusts were like unto horses prepared unto battle; and on their heads were as it were crowns like gold, and their faces were as the faces of men. And they had hair as the hair of women, and their teeth were as the teeth of lions. And they had breastplates, as it were breastplates of iron; and the sound of their wings was as the sound of chariots of many horses running to battle. And they had tails like unto scorpions, and there were stings in their tails: and their power was to hurt men five months. And they had a king over them, which is the angel of the bottomless pit, whose name in the Hebrew tongue is Abaddon, but in the Greek tongue hath his name Apollyon. One woe is past; and, behold, there come two woes more hereafter.*

The star in this case is an angel, being the guardian of the bottomless pit. He could be the same angel, Apollyon, named as their king, but as the [78]natural locust has no king, these cannot be natural locusts. The sun and moon are further darkened when the pit opens, and the locusts are revealed. These are not the usual locusts, as they have the power or sting of scorpions. Their mission is to hurt men; they are not sent to hurt the earth as real locusts would, by eating everything green! They target men who have not the seal of God, and their job is to inflict pain, rather than kill. They are limited in their power to just five months. It is difficult to imagine what these are, but their description as locusts may just refer to their vast numbers, and that everything in their path is destroyed. Notice that their power extends to those without the seal of God (and we know, for example that

---

78. See Proverbs 30:27, not needing leadership!

the one hundred and forty-four thousand are sealed), but there is no mention here of the mark of the Beast, as it is yet future to this event. Interestingly we are given the name of their [79]leader, Abbadon/Apollyon, which simply means 'destroyer'. The point to remember is that although they are kept in the bottomless pit, and are possibly fallen angels, they are nevertheless subject to God's will in this matter, through their king Apollyon, and cannot go beyond the range of their ministry.

The sixth trumpet, the second woe

Revelation 9:13-21: *And the sixth angel sounded, and I heard a voice from the four horns of the golden altar which is before God, Saying to the sixth angel which had the trumpet, Loose the four angels which are bound in the great river Euphrates. And the four angels were loosed, which were prepared for an hour, and a day, and a month, and a year, for to slay the third part of men. And the number of the army of the horsemen were two hundred thousand thousand: and I heard the number of them. And thus I saw the horses in the vision, and them that sat on them, having breastplates of fire, and of jacinth, and brimstone: and the heads of the horses were as the heads of lions; and out of their mouths issued fire and smoke and brimstone. By these three was the third part of men killed, by the fire, and by the smoke, and by the brimstone, which issued out of their mouths. For their power is in their mouth, and in their tails: for their tails were like unto serpents, and had heads, and with them they do hurt. And the rest of the men which were not killed by these plagues yet repented not of the works of their hands, that they should not worship devils, and idols of gold, and silver, and brass, and stone, and of wood: which neither can see, nor hear, nor walk: Neither repented they of their murders, nor of their sorceries, nor of their fornication, nor of their thefts.*

79. Some say this king is Satan himself, but there is no evidence for this.

The sounding of the sixth angel prompts a command from the horns of the altar in the heavens to let loose the four angels bound in the Euphrates. We are not told who these are, but if we appreciate that the Lord sent demons [80]underwater, then these may also have been bound in a similar way, requiring a commandment from this high level of authority to release them. The command is from the altar of incense, and may again refer to the prayers of the saints, combining with God's own will.

The translation here 'prepared for an hour, and a day, and a month, and a year' gives the wrong impression, and should be read as 'prepared for this very time', but they are restricted to killing the third of men. This is carried out by an army of two hundred million (myriads of myriads), described as horsemen, with fire, smoke and brimstone as their weapons to kill. The judgement seems to target those that worship devils, or idols, as well as those involved in murder, sorcery, fornication and theft. Sorcery originally meant medicines or drugs, and it could be that the combination of idol worship and its accompanying acts is targeted here. Another view could be that these are people involved in gangs, who promote such wickedness through their actions. In the light of previous judgements, law and order will be difficult to maintain at this time, and gang warfare might account for more than a few of the wicked. Amazingly, the purpose of these judgements is to bring men to repentance, but they still prefer to stay with what they have, even in the knowledge that they are bringing judgement down on themselves.

---

80. Matthew 8:31, the demons wanted to be cast into the swine, to continue to find other victims, but water seems to restrain them..

The seven thunders

Revelation 10:1-11: *And I saw another mighty angel come down from heaven, clothed with a cloud: and a rainbow was upon his head, and his face was as it were the sun, and his feet as pillars of fire. And he had in his hand a little book open: and he set his right foot upon the sea, and his left foot on the earth. And cried with a loud voice, as when a lion roareth: and when he had cried, seven thunders uttered their voices. And when the seven thunders had uttered their voices, I was about to write: and I heard a voice from heaven saying unto me, Seal up those things which the seven thunders uttered, and write them not. And the angel which I saw stand upon the sea and upon the earth lifted up his hand to heaven, And sware by Him that liveth for ever and ever, Who created heaven, and the things that therein are, and the earth, and the things that therein are, and the sea, and the things which are therein, that there should be time no longer: But in the days of the voice of the seventh angel, when he shall begin to sound, the mystery of God should be finished, as He hath declared to His servants the prophets. And the voice which I heard from heaven spake unto me again, and said, Go and take the little book which is open in the hand of the angel which standeth upon the sea and upon the earth. And I went unto the angel, and said unto him, Give me the little book. And he said unto me, Take it, and eat it up; and it shall make thy belly bitter, but it shall be in thy mouth sweet as honey. And I took the little book out of the angel's hand, and ate it up; and it was in my mouth sweet as honey: and as soon as I had eaten it, my belly was bitter. And he said unto me, Thou must prophesy again before many peoples, and nations, and tongues, and kings.*

In between the sixth and seventh trumpets we find two diversions from the main theme. Here it is an angel coming down from heaven to earth, holding a little book open. There is no suggestion that this is the same book as was in the Lord's hands, for this one is intended for John alone. Although it is not said here, the seven thunders seem to be uttered in response to the angel reading what is written in the book, and his crying out. John was commanded not to write what he had heard, but he did hear what the seven thunders had uttered, and did not question what he heard, so he probably understood it quite clearly. These seven thunders are not mentioned again, and their purpose is obscured deliberately. John is the central character connected with them, through having eaten the book that contains the record of what they were. This would suggest to me that John's ministry is a future one with close connection to the seven thunders. The next event mentioned may also relate to the seven thunders, being the second diversion from the main narrative and revealing the two witnesses, with whom John is also associated, being the one given the measuring rod.

The two witnesses

Revelation 11:1-14: *And there was given me a reed like unto a rod: and the angel stood, saying, Rise, and measure the temple of God, and the altar, and them that worship therein. But the court which is without the temple leave out, and measure it not; for it is given unto the Gentiles: and the holy city shall they tread under foot forty and two months. And I will give power unto my two witnesses, and they shall prophesy a thousand two hundred and threescore days, clothed in sackcloth. These are the two olive trees, and the two candlesticks standing before the God of the earth. And if any man will hurt them, fire proceedeth out of their mouth, and devoureth their enemies: and if any man will hurt them, he must in this manner be killed. These have power to shut heaven, that it rain not in the days of their prophecy: and have power over waters to turn them to blood, and to smite the earth with all plagues, as often as they will. And when they shall have finished their testimony, the Beast that ascendeth out of the bottomless pit shall make war against them, and shall overcome them, and kill them. And their dead bodies shall lie in the street of the great city, which spiritually is called Sodom and Egypt, where also our Lord was crucified. And they of the people and kindreds and tongues and nations shall see their dead bodies three days and an half, and shall not suffer their dead bodies to be put in graves. And they that dwell upon the earth shall rejoice over them, and make merry, and shall send gifts one to another; because these two prophets tormented them that dwelt on the earth. And after three days and an half the Spirit of life from God entered into them, and they stood upon their feet; and great fear fell upon them which saw them. And they heard a great voice from heaven saying unto them, Come up hither. And they ascended up to heaven in a cloud; and their enemies beheld them. And the same hour was there a great earthquake, and the tenth part of the city fell, and in the earthquake were slain of men seven thousand: and the remnant were affrighted, and gave glory to the God of heaven. The second woe is past; and, behold, the third woe cometh quickly.*

John's measuring rod covered those worshipping in the temple, or what passed for the temple in these times. Here we are given the two periods; the first, which is forty-two months, is the second period of the week, where the Gentiles are in control, treading Jerusalem under. The second period given is that of the ministry of the two witnesses, and their prophecy is limited to the same period of a 'thousand two hundred and sixty days', both periods combining to make the last seven years, or last week of Daniel's prophecy. As the Gentile domination of Israel can only be in the last period, it follows that the ministry of the two witnesses will take place in the first half of the week, and that at the end, when they have finished their prophecy, they are killed and resurrected. This is in the middle of the week, when they are in direct conflict with the 'Beast' that is to come, and this final event takes place in Jerusalem. Their deaths, proved by their bodies being on display, seems to be televised (or put on the internet) and sent round the world, to the rejoicing of those that that see it. Imagine their surprise when these are taken up, with the accompaniment of a great earthquake affecting Jerusalem.

Is it possible that the seven thousand killed there are believers, taken up with the two witnesses, as a form of 'remnant' as in the days of [81]Elijah? This is mere conjecture though, as we are not told why there are seven thousand in number. If we recognise that the two witnesses are ministering in the first half of the week, then some of the plagues earlier described in the trumpets could well be associated with them, as they are well able to demonstrate this sort of power. Clearly their acts and words are backed with God's authority, and no one can withstand them during the time of their ministry, which was a cause of torment to those on the earth. They seem to get the blame for what is happening by those who cannot accept their ministry, and the time given for repentance seems to diminish with their deaths.

These verses further demonstrate that the trumpets are not strictly chronological, for the ministry of these two is associated with the sixth trumpet, but commences at the start of the seven years. Notably though, the account of the thunders and the two witnesses are placed in the narrative before the seventh trumpet sounds and the final woe comes upon the earth.

There is an interesting comparison to be made with the two anointed ones of Zechariah 4 here, and we might also note the

81. 1 Kings 19:18.

connection with the seven spirits who are the eyes of the Lord that run to and fro throughout the whole earth. The two anointed ones seem to be the channel for the outpouring of the Spirit, through the seven spirits that stand before the throne. They hold an extremely high position, on a par with the cherubim themselves.

The seventh trumpet, the third woe

Revelation 11:15-19: *And the seventh angel sounded; and there were great voices in heaven, saying, The kingdoms of this world are become the kingdoms of our Lord, and of His Christ; and He shall reign for ever and ever. And the four and twenty elders, which sat before God on their seats, fell upon their faces, and worshipped God, Saying, We give Thee thanks, O Lord God Almighty, which art, and wast, and art to come; because Thou hast taken to Thee Thy great power, and hast reigned. And the nations were angry, and Thy wrath is come, and the time of the dead, that they should be judged, and that Thou shouldest give reward unto Thy servants the prophets, and to the saints, and them that fear Thy name, small and great; and shouldest destroy them which destroy the earth. And the temple of God was opened in heaven, and there was seen in His temple the ark of His testament: and there were lightnings, and voices, and thunderings, and an earthquake, and great hail.*

The sounding of the seventh trumpet is most significant, and seems to be what everyone in heaven is waiting for. When we consider what follows it - the man-child being take up, Satan being cast down to earth, the appearance of the Beast, the appearance of the False Prophet, the final persecutions of Israel and the appearance of the Lord as the Lamb - it is evident that these events are the culmination of much of the prophecy concerning the last days, or the Day of the Lord. I would mark the sounding of this trumpet as beginning the second half of the week, because although there is great rejoicing in heaven because of the trumpet which heralds the Lord's victory, events on the earth are about to get a whole lot tougher, especially for Israel itself.

The woman and the man-child

Revelation 12:1-4: *And there appeared a great wonder in heaven; a woman clothed with the sun, and the moon under her feet, and upon her head a crown of twelve stars: And she being with child cried, travailing in birth, and pained to be delivered. And there appeared another wonder in heaven; and behold a great red dragon, having seven heads and ten horns, and seven crowns upon his heads. And his tail drew the third part of the stars of heaven, and did cast them to the earth: and the dragon stood before the woman which was ready to be delivered, for to devour her child as soon as it was born.*

The woman is clearly, from her description, the nation Israel, not as a rebellious people here, but in its spiritual purpose, as the people of God on the earth. Now we see the enemy of Israel, the great red dragon, Satan, casting his followers to the earth in an attempt to destroy the man-child. Notably, it is the man-child that is the threat to Satan, for he is to rule the nations:

Revelation 12:5: *And she brought forth a man-child, who was to rule all nations with a rod of iron: and her child was caught up unto God, and to His throne.*

But the man-child is caught up to heaven before any harm can come to it. Many consider that the man-child is the Lord Himself, but He is the Son of God, not of Israel, and He has already come to earth, died, been resurrected and is in heaven already when this happens. Israel is the woman, feminine, so he/they (the man-child) are not Jewish, so the only reasonable conclusion is that the man-child is the Lord's Church, His heavenly body, which is not only expected to be made [82]manifest, but also to be called up to heaven, at the [83]'last trump'. The Church membership can lay claim to being the children of Abraham, and therefore be of the woman, by its [84]faith.

Revelation 12:6-17: *And the woman fled into the wilderness, where she hath a place prepared of God, that they should feed her there a thousand two hundred and threescore days. And there was war in heaven: Michael and his angels fought against the dragon; and the dragon fought and his angels, and prevailed not; neither was their place found any more in heaven. And the great dragon was cast out, that old serpent, called the Devil, and Satan, which deceiveth the whole world: he was cast out into the earth, and his angels were cast out with him. And I heard a loud voice saying in heaven, Now is come salvation, and strength, and the kingdom of our God, and the power of His Christ: for the accuser of our brethren is cast down, which accused them before our God day and night. And they overcame him by the blood of the Lamb, and by the word of their testimony; and they loved not their lives unto the death. Therefore rejoice, ye heavens, and ye that dwell in them. Woe to the inhabiters of the earth and of the sea! for the devil is come down unto you, having great wrath, because he knoweth that he hath but a short time. And when the dragon saw that he was cast unto the earth, he*

82. Romans 8:19.
83. 1 Corinthians 15:52.
84. Romans 4:11-16.

persecuted the woman which brought forth the man-child. And to the woman were given two wings of a great eagle, that she might fly into the wilderness, into her place, where she is nourished for a time, and times, and half a time, from the face of the serpent. And the serpent cast out of his mouth water as a flood after the woman, that he might cause her to be carried away of the flood. And the earth helped the woman, and the earth opened her mouth, and swallowed up the flood which the dragon cast out of his mouth. And the dragon was wroth with the woman, and went to make war with the remnant of her seed, which keep the commandments of God, and have the testimony of Jesus Christ.

After the rapture of the church, Satan further persecutes the Jews through his agent, the Beast. Note that Satan has now lost his place in heaven, and this suggests that when the church is taken up, he is revealed as the 'accuser of our brethren' and finally cast down, and his angels with him. This is the cause of all the rejoicing in heaven, for although he comes down to destroy Israel and try and prevent his own demise, the angels left in heaven can see that there is now an end to all his machinations and his heavenly authority. Whilst he still has power on earth, which he manifests through his man, the Beast, his days are numbered. He no longer has access to heaven.

Where the earth is concerned, this is the final 'woe' which is Satan's presence on the earth, intending to gain the worship of the world. He tries to wipe out the remainder of the believing Jews, and the remnant of her seed, who are probably those affected, and changed, by the ministry of the two witnesses. The means he uses are now described in more detail:

The Beast

Revelation 13:1-10: *And I stood upon the sand of the sea, and saw a Beast rise up out of the sea, having seven heads and ten horns, and upon his horns ten crowns, and upon his heads the name of blasphemy. And the Beast which I[85] saw was like unto a leopard, and his feet were as the feet of a bear, and his mouth as the mouth of a lion: and the dragon gave him his power, and his seat, and great authority. And I saw one of his heads as it were wounded to death; and his deadly wound was healed: and all the world wondered after the Beast. And they worshipped the dragon which gave power unto the Beast: and they worshipped the Beast, saying, Who is like unto the Beast? who is able to make war with him? And there was given unto him a mouth speaking great things and blasphemies; and power was given unto him to continue forty and two months. And he opened his mouth in blasphemy against God, to blaspheme His name, and His tabernacle, and them that dwell in heaven. And it was given unto him to make war with the saints, and to overcome them: and power was given him over all kindreds, and tongues, and nations. And all that dwell upon the earth shall worship him, whose names are not written in the book of life of the Lamb slain from the foundation of the world. If any man have an ear, let him hear. He that leadeth into captivity shall go into captivity: he that killeth with the sword must be killed with the sword. Here is the patience and the faith of the saints.*

The Beast is here described as the sum of the countries that he now dominates, as described in Daniel's account of the four beasts. He also displays the attributes of Satan, the great red dragon, as described earlier. This shows that the Beast now has power over all Satan's kingdom on the earth, bringing his

85. This is a composite picture of the four beasts of Daniel 7. The Beast completely dominates the other three here.

apparent power and dominion to visible display. He also has the marks of having died, but we do not know exactly when this has happened, only that he has somehow been raised again.

This fact, coupled with his obvious power through the ten-kingdom confederation, causes the world to be deceived into believing that he is their Messiah, and they offer their worship. His time is now limited to the last three and a half years of the final week, but during this period he becomes even more emboldened by his own success. The focus of his ranting is towards Israel and their God, and he gives the appearance of being an authority on these things, his blasphemy even reaching to the heavens, where angels no doubt are wondering for just how long he will get away with it. In these times there is little chance of repentance; people have made their decisions, and as they have not accepted the truth, they are deceived into believing the lie concerning the Beast, that he is indeed their awaited saviour, and is God, as he claims.

The False Prophet

Revelation 13:11-18: *And I beheld another beast coming up out of the earth; and he had two horns like a lamb, and he spake as a dragon. And he exerciseth all the power of the first Beast before him, and causeth the earth and them which dwell therein to worship the first Beast, whose deadly wound was healed. And he doeth great wonders, so that he maketh fire come down from heaven on the earth in the sight of men, And deceiveth them that dwell on the earth by the means of those miracles which he had power to do in the sight of the Beast; saying to them that dwell on the earth, that they should make an image to the Beast, which had the wound by a sword, and did live. And he had power to give life unto the image of the Beast, that the image of the Beast should both speak, and cause that as many as would not worship the image of the Beast should be killed. And he causeth all, both small and great, rich and poor, free and bond, to receive a mark in their right hand, or in their foreheads: And that no man might buy or sell, save he that had the mark, or the name of the Beast, or the number of his name. Here is wisdom. Let him that hath understanding count the number of the Beast: for it is the number of a man; and his number is Six hundred threescore and six.*

From the way he is described in scripture, it seems that the Beast starts off as a statesman and negotiator, using his talents to secure a deal with Israel that will also be acceptable to the Arab nations, who are directly affected. He also turns his energies to gathering together first three, then ten kingdoms that he can use to subdue the Middle East and beyond. In addition, his kingdom begins to extend to the other three beasts that are associated with the former Empires, Babylon, Persia and Greece (Syria). It is only in the latter stages, perhaps from the middle of the week onwards, from his direct involvement with Satan, and following the introduction of this further character, the second Beast the False Prophet, that he becomes interested in being the focus of worship, becoming convinced that he is 'God'. Just who this second Beast is and where he comes from is not revealed, but we do know that he has two horns 'like a lamb', which suggests he is a religious leader who looks the part, and also that he speaks as a dragon, ie Satan, who himself appears as an angel of light to men.

The likelihood is that he represents one or several large religious groups and is able to persuade others of the integrity of the Beast, presenting him as a 'Messiah or Mahdi' figure to the world. Moreover, this second beast is involved in setting up the image to the Beast, which is probably the 'abomination of desolation' Daniel and the Lord spoke of, and then he forces people to worship it, with the option of death if they refuse. He is also responsible for the mark of the Beast being implemented as the means to buy or trade.

A popular interpretation of this character sees him as a future Pope of the Roman Catholic Church, but later descriptions of the involvement of Babylon and its prosperity and worship in these last day events suggest to me that he is more likely to be a representative of a form of worship directly connected to Babylon or Iraq, and that it becomes very much in the interests of Babylon to promote the Beast as the head of its religion. Certainly Iraq, or Babylon, is to come to great prominence through trade with other nations at this future time and its hatred of Israel is well known. Something has to occur to substantially increase Iraq's power and influence in the future, for at present, it is an increasingly troubled country. This is also true for Syria, Turkey, and Iran, its three contemporaries, depicted as beasts, in the end times.

The Lamb

Revelation 14:1–5: *And I looked, and, lo, a Lamb stood on the mount Sion, and with Him an hundred forty and four thousand, having His Father's name written in their foreheads. And I heard a voice from heaven, as the voice of many waters, and as the voice of a great thunder: and I heard the voice of harpers harping with their harps: And they sung as it were a new song before the throne, and before the four beasts, and the elders: and no man could learn that song but the hundred and forty and four thousand, which were redeemed from the earth. These are they which were not defiled with women; for they are virgins. These are they which follow the Lamb whithersoever He goeth. These were redeemed from among men, being the firstfruits unto God and to the Lamb. And in their mouth was found no guile: for they are without fault before the throne of God.*

We remember that between the opening of the sixth and the seventh seal there was a group of 144,000 sealed to go through the great tribulation, and here they are seen again, sealed with the name of the Father on their foreheads. They have a 'new song,' that is played by the harpers but that only they can learn. The experience that they have to learn is exclusive to them, but in the context of later [86]verses this could well be in anticipation of victory, in a similar vein to Moses' song, written in praise of the Lord delivering His people from the Egyptians. The Lord and His 144,000 are set here in contrast with the forces of Satan, personified in the Beast and the False Prophet, and what we probably have described in the last few verses is the 'order of battle', a description of the main protagonists involved, setting the scene before the events of the last three and a half years occur.

Revelation 14:6-7: *And I saw another angel fly in the midst of heaven, having the everlasting gospel to preach unto them that dwell on the earth, and to every nation, and kindred, and tongue, and people, Saying with a loud voice, Fear God, and give glory to Him; for the hour of His judgment is come: and worship Him that made heaven, and earth, and the sea, and the fountains of waters.*

Whether the everlasting gospel relates to the song that the 144,000 learn is conjecture, but there is clearly a final appeal to the world to consider their actions before it is too late, and resist

86. Revelation 15:3, see also Psalm 98.

the temptation to worship the Beast, or accept his mark, which will shortly bring certain judgement down upon them. The hundred and forty-four thousand may well be the heralds of this everlasting gospel, which will be the one preached from now on, that of God's kingdom being established on the earth through His people Israel.

Revelation 14:8-11: *And there followed another angel, saying, Babylon is fallen, is fallen, that great city, because she made all nations drink of the wine of the wrath of her fornication. And the third angel followed them, saying with a loud voice, If any man worship the Beast and his image, and receive his mark in his forehead, or in his hand, The same shall drink of the wine of the wrath of God, which is poured out without mixture into the cup of His indignation; and he shall be tormented with fire and brimstone in the presence of the holy angels, and in the presence of the Lamb: And the smoke of their torment ascendeth up for ever and ever: and they have no rest day nor night, who worship the Beast and his image, and whosoever receiveth the mark of his name.*

The judgement of Babylon is closely associated with the mark of the Beast, and this may give a clue as to what the 'wine of the wrath of her fornication' is, for these are the judgements of God which closely follow in this final period. It seems that Babylon is the cause of all nations partaking of judgement, through 'her fornication'. Although we could take this in a traditional and literal sense, it is more likely that the word 'fornication' relates more to spiritual apostasy from God, and there can be little doubt that Babylon will now be under the control of Satan himself, as the nation through which he is operating to try and hasten the destruction of the Jews in these end times. He is described as the King of Babylon in [87]Isaiah, and the destruction of Babylon at the hands of the ten [88]kingdoms is a prelude to the final destruction of the Beast and the False Prophet, which signals the end of the final three and a half year period.

Revelation 14:12-20: *Here is the patience of the saints: here are they that keep the commandments of God, and the faith of Jesus. And I heard a voice from heaven saying unto me, Write, Blessed are the dead which die in the Lord from henceforth: Yea, saith the Spirit, that they may rest from their labours; and their works do follow them. And I looked, and behold a white cloud, and upon the cloud one sat like unto the Son of Man, having on His head a golden crown, and in His hand a sharp sickle. And another angel came out of the temple, crying with a loud voice to Him that sat on the cloud, Thrust in Thy sickle, and reap: for the time is come for Thee to reap; for the harvest of the earth is ripe. And he that sat on the cloud thrust in His sickle on the earth; and the earth was reaped. And another angel came out of the temple which is in heaven, he also having a sharp sickle. And another angel came out from the altar, which had power over fire; and cried with a loud cry to him that had the sharp sickle, saying, Thrust in thy sharp sickle, and gather the clusters of the vine of the earth; for her grapes are fully ripe. And the angel thrust in his sickle into the earth, and gathered the vine of the earth, and cast it into the great winepress of the wrath of God. And the winepress was trodden without the city, and blood came out of the winepress, even unto the horse bridles, by the space of a thousand and six hundred furlongs.*

87. Isaiah 14:4-23.
88. Revelation 17:16-18.

The Jews though, until this time, are expected to remain faithful, and clearly there are many, both Jews and Gentiles, killed during this time for their refusal to submit to the Beast, or his image. However, this is the time of God's retribution on the earth, seen through the actions of the two angels who perform the killing. The extent of the deaths is indicated through the description of the blood being up to the horse bridles and extending over sixteen hundred furlongs, about 182 miles.

CHAPTER ELEVEN

THE SEVEN VIALS, THE WRATH OF GOD

✵

Revelation 15:1-8: *And I saw another sign in heaven, great and marvellous, seven angels having the seven last plagues; for in them is filled up the wrath of God. And I saw as it were a sea of glass mingled with fire: and them that had gotten the victory over the Beast, and over his image, and over his mark, and over the number of his name, stand on the sea of glass, having the harps of God. And they sing the song of Moses the servant of God, and the song of the Lamb, saying, Great and marvellous are Thy works, Lord God Almighty; just and true are Thy ways, Thou King of saints. Who shall not fear Thee, O Lord, and glorify Thy name? for Thou only art holy: for all nations shall come and worship before Thee; for Thy judgments are made manifest. And after that I looked, and, behold, the temple of the tabernacle of the testimony in heaven was opened: And the seven angels came out of the temple, having the seven plagues, clothed in pure and white linen, and having their breasts girded with golden girdles. And one of the four beasts gave unto the seven angels seven golden vials full of the wrath of God, Who liveth for ever and ever. And the temple was filled with smoke from the glory of God, and from His power; and no man was able to enter into the temple, till the seven plagues of the seven angels were fulfilled.*

Now is the beginning of the end of the last week, for these are the seven last plagues, that will see out the three and a half year period, having the wrath of God 'filled up', or completed. We also see those that had gotten the victory over the Beast, through having resisted his mark or image. This has probably cost them their lives, and they are now seen in heaven before the throne, in victory. They also proclaim that all nations will now submit to the Lord's righteousness, His judgements having been made manifest, but this is a jump forward in time, and yet in the future. Before this happens the seven angels must perform their ministry, for no one can enter into worship in the temple until this is done.

Revelation 16:1-2: *And I heard a great voice out of the temple saying to the seven angels, Go your ways, and pour out the vials of the wrath of God upon the earth. And the first went, and poured out his vial upon the earth; and there fell a noisome and grievous sore upon the men which had the mark of the Beast, and upon them which worshipped his image.*

Out of the vial, or shallow bowl, comes the plague of ulcers, and this comes specifically on those with the mark of the Beast, or his worshippers.

Revelation 16:3: *And the second angel poured out his vial upon the sea; and it became as the blood of a dead man: and every living soul died in the sea.*

The second plague comes on the seas, turning them as the blood of a dead man, that is, full of disease, as from a corpse. This causes all that is in the sea to die, fish, mammals, etc., but not plant life.

Revelation 16:4-7: *And the third angel poured out his vial upon the rivers and fountains of waters; and they became blood. And I heard the angel of the waters say, Thou art righteous, O Lord, which art, and wast, and shalt be, because Thou hast judged thus. For they have shed the blood of saints and prophets, and Thou hast given them blood to drink; for they are worthy. And I heard another out of the altar say, Even so, Lord God Almighty, true and righteous are Thy judgments.*

The rivers and fountains of waters, drinking waters, are now turned to blood, and we are not told what the effect of this is. Although the waters can still be taken, they must taste terrible!

Revelation 16:8-9: *And the fourth angel poured out his vial upon the sun; and power was given unto him to scorch men with fire. And men were scorched with great heat, and blasphemed the name of God, which hath power over these plagues: and they repented not to give Him glory.*

Any change to the sun will cause abnormalities to this earth's atmosphere, and this seems to be what is involved here. In nature this must have already been set up in the sun's life cycle being timed to occur at this particular point in God's will. This will also be true for the sun's total destruction later. This plague causes blasphemy, but is intended to bring men to repentance, for God is perfectly able to control the plagues, even as He can the sun, and He would stop these things happening if men would return to Him. If we recall the sixth seal, the angels are holding back the winds, and such heat would also destroy trees, taking out shade, which means there would be no relief from the sun's rays.

Revelation 16:10-11: *And the fifth angel poured out his vial upon the seat of the Beast; and his kingdom was full of darkness; and they gnawed their tongues for pain, And blasphemed the God of heaven because of their pains and their sores, and repented not of their deeds.*

Scripturally Satan gives his seat to the Beast, and this seat is named as Pergamos, which is situated very near to Istanbul, in modern-day Turkey. If we suppose that his kingdom is Turkey, which is the remnant of the former Roman Empire, then we see where this darkness will emanate from. Of course, the Beast is complex, and may have established himself elsewhere. In either case, this is a bleak forewarning of his coming failure, for it is those who are his most ardent supporters who are now suffering, yet they still refuse to accept that it is a result of God's judgement on them for their support of the Beast. Darkness is a feature of the whole of the last week, volcanic and seismic events on earth conspiring to block out what light there is. For all the miraculous powers the Beast and the False Prophet display, they are not capable of preventing these things happening.

Revelation 16:12-16: *And the sixth angel poured out his vial upon the great river Euphrates; and the water thereof was dried up, that the way of the kings of the east might be prepared. And I saw three unclean spirits like frogs come out of the mouth of the dragon, and out of the mouth of the Beast, and out of the mouth of the False Prophet. For they are the spirits of devils, working miracles, which go forth unto the kings of the earth and of the whole world, to gather them to the battle of that great day of God Almighty. Behold, I come as a thief. Blessed is he that watcheth, and keepeth his garments, lest he walk naked, and they see his shame. And he gathered them together into a place called in the Hebrew tongue Armageddon.*

The drying up of the river Euphrates seems to suggest that the river is a barrier to a modern army, which is not the case. More relevant is the fact that the Euphrates begins in Turkey, and flows through both Syria and Iraq. It is a vital source of water to all three countries, and if it should dry up, there would be terrible hardship in these countries. There are presently agreements in place concerning the amount of water allowed to flow from Turkey, and if these supplies are interrupted for any reason, then it is conceivable that they would go to war in order to obtain water to both drink and irrigate crops. It is possible that Turkey itself would stop the water flow, especially if good drinking water is becoming scarcer. This seems quite reasonable, in view of the fact that the nations are being drawn together for judgement at Armageddon. The Lord reminds the faithful that in their darkest hour, when all seems lost, He will appear.

We are not told who these armies are assembled to fight with and I have always assumed that it is Israel. However, Israel is at this time under the control of the Beast, so the conflict must be between other great armies, possibly between Babylon and others, against the forces of the [89]Beast, with Israel caught somewhere in the middle. This is the time when the Lord will destroy many, and the exhortation once again is to the faithful to be watchful. The unwary are compared to the old Jewish Temple guards, who if found asleep at night by an officer were likely to have their clothes set on fire, and then have to appear publicly the next day in their burnt rags, for further humiliating judgement.

Revelation 16:17-21: *And the seventh angel poured out his vial into the air; and there came a great voice out of the temple of heaven, from the throne, saying, It is done. And there were voices, and thunders, and*

---

89. The Lord talks about 'My great army' the 'Northern army,' Joel 2:20-25, and we know that the ten kingdom confederation are there to do His will and destroy Babylon, Revelation 17:16-17.

lightnings; and there was a great earthquake, such as was not since men were upon the earth, so mighty an earthquake, and so great. And the great city was divided into three parts, and the cities of the nations fell: and great Babylon came in remembrance before God, to give unto her the cup of the wine of the fierceness of His wrath. And every island fled away, and the mountains were not found. And there fell upon men a great hail out of heaven, every stone about the weight of a talent: and men blasphemed God because of the plague of the hail; for the plague thereof was exceeding great.

The final vial is poured out into the air, and this provokes *'voices, thunders, lightnings, and a great earthquake'*; nothing like it having been seen before for magnitude. The country most affected seems to be [90]Babylon, which is divided into three, but other cities are not exempt either. The earth's topography is changed in these events, and phenomena such as this hail are produced, which cause further blasphemy.

The Great Whore, and the marriage supper of the Lamb

Revelation 17:1-18: *And there came one of the seven angels which had the seven vials, and talked with me saying unto me, Come hither; I will shew unto thee the judgment of the great whore that sitteth upon many waters: With whom the kings of the earth have committed fornication, and the inhabitants of the earth have been made drunk with the wine of her fornication. So he carried me away in the spirit into the wilderness: and I saw a woman sit upon a scarlet coloured Beast, full of names of blasphemy, having seven heads and ten horns. And the woman was arrayed in purple and scarlet colour, and decked with gold and*

---

90. Of course the city of Babylon does not exist at present, only as an historical site. We must assume that either it is completely restored, or that The Scriptures refer to the whole country of Iraq when referring to Babylon. The language used seems to suggest Babylon as a city.

precious stones and pearls, having a golden cup in her hand full of abominations and filthiness of her fornication: And upon her forehead was a name written, *MYSTERY, BABYLON THE GREAT, THE MOTHER OF HARLOTS AND ABOMINATIONS OF THE EARTH*. And I saw the woman drunken with the blood of the saints, and with the blood of the martyrs of Jesus: and when I saw her, I wondered with great admiration. And the angel said unto me, Wherefore didst thou marvel? I will tell thee the mystery of the woman, and of the Beast that carrieth her, which hath the seven heads and ten horns. The Beast that thou sawest was, and is not; and shall ascend out of the bottomless pit, and go into perdition: and they that dwell on the earth shall wonder, whose names were not written in the book of life from the foundation of the world, when they behold the Beast that was, and is not, and yet is.

And here is the mind which hath wisdom. The seven heads are seven mountains, on which the woman sitteth. And there are seven kings: five are fallen, and one is, and the other is not yet come; and when he cometh, he must continue a short space. And the Beast that was, and is not, even he is the eighth, and is of the seven, and goeth into perdition. And the ten horns which thou sawest are ten kings, which have received no kingdom as yet; but receive power as kings one hour with the Beast. These have one mind, and shall give their power and strength unto the Beast. These shall make war with the Lamb, and the Lamb shall overcome them: for He is Lord of lords, and King of kings: and they that are with Him are called, and chosen, and faithful. And he saith unto me, The waters which thou sawest, where the whore sitteth, are peoples, and multitudes, and nations, and tongues. And the ten horns which thou sawest upon the Beast, these shall hate the whore, and shall make her desolate and naked, and shall eat her flesh, and burn her with fire. For God hath put in their hearts to fulfil His will, and to agree, and give their kingdom unto the Beast, until the words of God shall be fulfilled.

And the woman which thou sawest is that great city, which reigneth over the kings of the earth.

It is difficult to determine exactly when Babylon is destroyed, but it is probably near to the end of events of the last week, and connected to the last vial. There is a lot of time devoted to the description of its downfall, and from this we see that the Lord holds Babylon accountable for both the fornication (apostasy) of the world from Him, and the persecutions of His nation Israel. Although He set out to judge the nation Israel for its rejection of Himself, this is now over, and He begins dealing with its enemies, ironically using Satan's kingdom to turn in on itself. In effect the Lord does very little, He has "sat down at the right hand of God, expecting His enemies to become His footstool", and sure enough, Satan's kingdom is divided and cannot stand. In the description, both the woman and the Beast on which she sits are associated with scarlet and purple, the clothing of the rulers, and the rich. The Beast has the seven heads and ten horns, and is full of the names of blasphemy, but it is the woman who is now in control, riding on the Beast. The woman is given the pre-eminence in judgement as the *'mother of harlots, and abominations in the earth'* and this title reflects the enmity between her, and the Lord's faithful, that she set out to destroy.

The explanation is given of the Beast first, who although his earthly power comes from the ten, has died and been resurrected. This is what is meant by "was, and is not, even he is the eighth, and is of the seven, and goeth into perdition." The world must learn of his being restored to life, and be suitably impressed. Traditionally the seven mountains on which the woman sits are interpreted as meaning Rome, the city, and this seems to fit, as it is from within the boundaries of the Roman

Empire, in its last stages, that the Beast draws his power, which are the 'legs and feet of iron, mixed with the miry clay' of Nebuchadnezzar's dream. This kingdom was diverse from the other three, and subdued them.

The seven kings are a little more difficult to identify, but must succeed each other from the description given. If we assume that they are Roman, the one that is, relative to John's time, is Domitian, and the one that is not yet come is the Beast in his first incarnation (the seventh), who then dies and is raised up to become the eighth. This would make him of the seven, and then fit the description. Who the five previous Roman rulers are is a matter for discussion, but it may be that they are Roman rulers before John's time, promoting the Imperial Cult, who also demanded worship, setting themselves up as gods as the Beast does in his final appearance. The ten kingdoms are more difficult to identify, but must come from within the Roman Empire, as it once was. Rome at its height encompassed most of Europe, Turkey, Babylon, Israel, and Egypt, and also extended along the North coast of Africa, giving a wide choice of nations from which the Ten could be drawn.

As this Ten Kingdom confederation was diverse from the others, and does not appear in power until the Beast is in control, ruling with him for one 'hour' at the end period, it may not be apparent, until later in the week, just who the kings are. It could also be that these are religious or tribal leaders, not necessarily having countries at all, but groups of followers. Whoever they are, they develop great military might and expertise, and are ruthless in their approach in subjugating others, as were the original Roman legions. Eventually these are used by the Lord to destroy the 'Whore, Babylon', but then are destroyed themselves by the Lord for their opposition to Him against

Israel. Clearly the 'Beast', where the whore sits, is in control of more than one nation at this time, and we can only guess at what causes the rift between Babylon and the Ten. My own view is that Babylon becomes rich through its association with the name, mark or image of the Beast, and that there is some form of taxation or trading licence involved, of which Babylon is the main beneficiary. The Beast and the ten kingdoms he rules, might regard this as disproportionate? This would explain in part, the Whore riding on the Beast.

Revelation 18:1-24: *And after these things I saw another angel come down from heaven, having great power; and the earth was lightened with his glory. And he cried mightily with a strong voice, saying, Babylon the great is fallen, is fallen, and is become the habitation of devils, and the hold of every foul spirit, and a cage of every unclean and hateful bird. For all nations have drunk of the wine of the wrath of her fornication, and the kings of the earth have committed fornication with her, and the merchants of the earth are waxed rich through the abundance of her delicacies. And I heard another voice from heaven, saying, Come out of her, My people, that ye be not partakers of her sins, and that ye receive not of her plagues. For her sins have reached unto heaven, and God hath remembered her iniquities. Reward her even as she rewarded you, and double unto her double according to her works: in the cup which she hath filled fill to her double. How much she hath glorified herself, and lived deliciously, so much torment and sorrow give her: for she saith in her heart, I sit a [91]queen, and am no widow, and shall see no sorrow.*

91. This reveals that Babylon sees itself as married, but who is her king? It could be Satan himself, but he is seen later directly connected in his incitement of Gog and Magog. A more likely possibility is that Babylon is tied to, and protected by, the beast and his ten kingdom confederation, from whom she has become rich. This union ends in disaster when the ten turn on her. Here is an attempt by Satan to offer a substitute people to the world, masquerading as God's people, yet intent on destroying the rightful heirs. For a while, the world is deceived into believing the lie! Contrast this with the marriage of the Lamb to His bride Israel, the description of which follows after the destruction of Babylon. The strong language used of Babylon, as the 'whore' shows that its real motive is money and power, there is no sentiment or faithfulness involved here, whichever way it chooses to depict itself!

Therefore shall her plagues come in one day, death, and mourning, and famine; and she shall be utterly burned with fire: for strong is the Lord God Who judgeth her. And the kings of the earth, who have committed fornication and lived deliciously with her, shall bewail her, and lament for her, when they shall see the smoke of her burning, Standing afar off for the fear of her torment, saying, Alas, alas, that great city Babylon, that mighty city! for in one hour is thy judgment come. And the merchants of the earth shall weep and mourn over her; for no man buyeth their merchandise any more: The merchandise of gold, and silver, and precious stones, and of pearls, and fine linen, and purple, and silk, and scarlet, and all thyine wood, and all manner vessels of ivory, and all manner vessels of most precious wood, and of brass, and iron, and marble, And cinnamon, and odours, and ointments, and frankincense, and wine, and oil, and fine flour, and wheat, and beasts, and sheep, and horses, and chariots, and slaves, and souls of men. And the fruits that thy soul lusted after are departed from thee, and all things which were dainty and goodly are departed from thee, and thou shalt find them no more at all. The merchants of these things, which were made rich by her, shall stand afar off for the fear of her torment, weeping and wailing, And saying, Alas, alas, that great city, that was clothed in fine linen, and purple, and scarlet, and decked with gold, and precious stones, and pearls! For in one hour so great riches is come to nought. And every shipmaster, and all the company in ships, and sailors, and as many as trade by sea, stood afar off, And cried when they saw the smoke of her burning, saying, What city is like unto this great city! And they cast dust on their heads, and cried, weeping and wailing, saying, Alas, alas, that great city, wherein were made rich all that had ships in the sea by reason of her costliness! for in one hour is she made desolate. Rejoice over her, thou heaven, and ye holy apostles and prophets; for God hath avenged you on her. And a mighty angel took up a stone like a great millstone, and cast it into the sea, saying, Thus with violence shall that great city Babylon be thrown down, and shall be found no more at all. And the voice of harpers, and musicians, and of pipers, and trumpeters, shall be heard no more at all in thee; and no craftsman, of whatsoever craft he be, shall be found any more in thee; and the sound of a millstone shall be heard no more at all in thee; And the light of a candle shall shine no more at all in thee; and the voice of the bridegroom and of the bride shall be heard no more at all in thee: for thy merchants were the great men of the earth; for by thy sorceries were all nations deceived. And in her was found the blood of prophets, and of saints, and of all that were slain upon the earth.

The desolations of Babylon are the cause of much rejoicing in heavenly terms, but the source of mourning for the kings and merchants who have benefited from its great wealth. At the time of writing Iraq is in turmoil, being occupied in part by rebel groups in opposition to its government. This is also true for Syria and Egypt, with Turkey also being subject to active dissent and rebellion. There must be a future time of stability to come for all these nations, for them to build such power and wealth, and these are perhaps the problems that the 'Beast' addresses, offering a resolution that eventually unifies the four great 'Empires' of the latter day images written of by Daniel. Those Jews or other believers remaining in Babylon at this time, whether voluntarily or as slaves, are exhorted to flee from the destruction to come, as there is a danger of them being caught up in it. Again, the watchful and the undecided among the people can be saved, but the mockers will stay, and be destroyed. Notice that the sorrow for Babylon is for themselves and the financial loss that Babylon's destruction will cause them. This reveals that the motive for both Babylon and those who affected by its fall is material gain. There is no mention of repentance for the spiritual departure from the rule of God at all, or for the persecution of Israel. Regardless of whatever religion these peoples then profess, the worship of the Beast encourages material gain. Everything else is secondary to this.

Again, Babylon is [92]judged for its deception of the earth through its 'sorceries' (the root meaning of which is 'medication or drugs') and by implication, witchcraft or magic. Babylonians were known to be expert in interpreting the signs of the Zodiac, so astrology or predicting the future could also play a part in its end day rise to prominence. Its destruction is sudden, and by fire, and seems to come at the hands of the 'ten' who are used in God's will to destroy it. Whether this is a nuclear explosion or not, remains to be seen, but such sudden wholesale destruction is well within the scope of a modern well-equipped army; Israel is under occupation, and may have lost its nuclear arsenal to the Beast at this time.

Revelation 19:1-21: *And after these things I heard a great voice of much people in heaven, saying, Alleluia; Salvation, and glory, and honour, and power, unto the Lord our God: For true and righteous are His judgments: for He hath judged the great whore, which did corrupt the earth with her fornication, and hath avenged the blood of His servants at her hand. And again they said, Alleluia. And her smoke rose up for ever and ever. And the four and twenty elders and the four beasts fell down and worshipped God that sat on the throne, saying, Amen; Alleluia. And a voice came out of the throne, saying, Praise our God, all ye His servants, and ye that fear Him, both small and great. And I heard as it were the voice of a great multitude, and as the voice of many waters, and as the voice of mighty thunderings, saying, Alleluia: for the Lord God omnipotent reigneth. Let us be glad and rejoice, and give honour to Him: for the marriage of the Lamb is come, and His wife*

92. See also Isaiah 47:9.

hath made herself ready. And to her was granted that she should be arrayed in fine linen, clean and white: for the fine linen is the righteousness of saints. And he saith unto me, Write, Blessed are they which are called unto the marriage supper of the Lamb.

And he saith unto me, These are the true sayings of God. And I fell at his feet to worship him. And he said unto me, See thou do it not: I am thy fellowservant, and of thy brethren that have the testimony of Jesus: worship God: for the testimony of Jesus is the spirit of prophecy. And I saw heaven opened, and behold a white horse; and He that sat upon Him was called Faithful and True, and in righteousness He doth judge and make war. His eyes were as a flame of fire, and on His head were many crowns; and He had a name written, that no man knew, but He Himself. And He was clothed with a vesture dipped in blood: and His name is called The Word of God. And the armies which were in heaven followed Him upon white horses, clothed in fine linen, white and clean. And out of His mouth goeth a sharp sword, that with it He should smite the nations: and He shall rule them with a rod of iron: and He treadeth the winepress of the fierceness and wrath of Almighty God. And He hath on His vesture and on His thigh a name written, KING OF KINGS, AND LORD OF LORDS. And I saw an angel [93] standing in the sun; and He cried with a loud voice, saying to all the fowls that fly in the midst of heaven, Come and gather yourselves together unto the supper of the great God; That ye may eat the flesh of kings, and the flesh of captains, and the flesh of mighty men, and the flesh of horses, and of them that sit on them, and the flesh of all men, both free and bond, both small and great. And I saw the Beast, and the kings of the earth, and their armies, gathered together to make war against Him that sat on the horse, and against His army. And the Beast was taken, and with him the False Prophet that wrought miracles before him, with which

93. The angel in the sun would also block out the light of both the sun and the moon, which is another feature of the end of the final week.

194

he deceived them that had received the mark of the Beast, and them that worshipped his image. These both were cast alive into a lake of fire burning with brimstone. And the remnant were slain with the sword of Him that sat upon the horse, which sword proceeded out of His mouth: and all the fowls were filled with their flesh.

Again, the whore, or Babylon, is given direct blame for perpetrating the myth of the Beast, and causing the slaughter of many of the Jews. These judgements are clearly seen in heavenly places as a cause of rejoicing, and contrast with the reaction of the world to its destruction, which is in mourning because it has lost a profitable source of income. The judgement of Babylon paves the way for the forthcoming marriage of the Lamb, and His [94]bride, Israel, is seen as prepared, having 'made herself ready,' through waiting to be joined finally to the Lord, as The Messiah.

Those 'called' are seen in their appearance with the Lord as His [95]army, when He comes as the groom. Jewish wedding preparations are more complex than our own, and the marriage supper commences when the groom appears at the bride's home to bring her back to the place he has prepared. The exact timing of this is not known, and is decided by the father of the groom, when he is satisfied that everything prior to the event has been completed properly. This is why Israel, as the bride, was told by the Lord when He was on earth to be ready for His coming, having been given the promise of His return for them, but not the exact time. They are expected to know from the [96]signs

94. The many reference in our bible headings, particularly in the Old Testament, referring to the 'church' as the bride, can be safely ignored. The 'church' was not known of in Old Testament times, it was hidden, a mystery, revealed when Israel itself rejected the Lord at the end of the Acts period. Paul writing in Romans and Ephesians, covers this fully. Here in Revelation scripture is talking of Israel starting to take up its rightful place to be united as one with the Lord.

95. There must be others also, Gentiles, who have watched events take place, and realised the injustice dealt out to Israel through the operations of the Beast, the False Prophet, and Satan, working through the ten kingdoms, the four empires, and Babylon. The importance of the ministry of the two witnesses cannot be overestimated, and to those that look for it, there will be every encouragement to believe the truth, regardless of the various attempts of Satan to deceive.

96. Matthew 16:2-4.

roughly when this should take place, and the more observant will have read their scriptures and be able to put two and two together. The wicked, of course, will have no signs to enlighten them at all, as they are deceived! The marriage supper itself begins when groom appears at the house of the intended with his entourage, having made his way through the streets with his friends. When near, they sound the *shofar* or trumpet to announce their presence, and the bride and her friends are then taken to the grooms' father's house. As part of the supper the groom makes vows or promises to his wife-to-be, and the celebrations begin.

The actual marriage ceremony will have taken place any time up to a year previously, and consisted of a contract, or covenant, being made with the bride at her father's house, sealed by the drinking of a cup of wine. The period thereafter, until the marriage proper, is called the [97]betrothal, and is as binding in Jewish eyes as the physical consummation of the marriage itself. If the groom wished to change his mind during this period, an actual divorce had to be obtained. It is during the period between the contract and the marriage supper that the bride waits, and the bridegroom prepares a place in 'his father's house' for them to live. The father of the groom has to approve the home made before he will allow the marriage to be consummated.

The marriage supper precedes the physical union of bride and groom, but the important thing in Jewish law is the initial making of the contract/covenant, which always involves paying a price. This is why the bride, or Israel, is called the Lamb's wife, for His sacrifice on the cross is the price paid for the bride, Israel!

---

97. We would call this an engagement, but it does not carry the same weight in our society.

We can see in this passage that those invited to partake in the celebrations are invited, along with the fowls of heaven to 'eat the flesh of kings'; this is the feast provided, with the promise to Israel that its enemies will never again overcome it, as the Lord will defend it from now on. We have yet to see the marriage, which is described later, but the Lord returning to Israel as the groom on the white horse, providing a feast for His faithful, anticipates the marriage to come.

These truths so overcome John that he bows down to the angel who is guiding him. The angel refuses his worship, indicating that he is also a fellow servant with John, having the [98]testimony of the Lord, and is therefore a man. It is curious that John offers worship, but perhaps in the heat of the moment he may have mistaken him for the Lord, due to the power displayed here.

The Lord in His true glory is now revealed to John sitting on a white horse, not as an imposter, as the rider of the first seal was, but the real thing, the Word of God. We can include ourselves, as His Church or body, in the armies which followed Him, and are present at this final battle, with the Beast and the kings of the earth drawn together for their destruction. His title, King of kings and Lord of lords, shows that despite the display of strength and power that Satan had enabled, all of these nations and armies, with their intention to dominate the earth, are subject to God's will, and are there at His command. The destruction here is total, all sides are wiped out, and this is the culmination of the winepress of the wrath of God, the seventh vial. Both the Beast and the False Prophet are cast into the lake of fire; their judgement is already decided, the Lord has no further use for them and there is no hope for them of ever

---

98. Testimony = Gr: marturia, from where we get our word 'martyr'. All too often the testimony of the Lord involves the death of the messenger, as may be the case here!

coming out of this place of torment. They have knowingly given themselves over to wickedness, and are given no further opportunity to state their case.

Revelation 20:1-15: *And I saw an angel come down from heaven, having the key of the bottomless pit and a great chain in his hand. And he laid hold on the dragon, that old serpent, which is the Devil, and Satan, and bound him a thousand years, And cast him into the bottomless pit, and shut him up, and set a seal upon him, that he should deceive the nations no more, till the thousand years should be fulfilled: and after that he must be loosed a little season. And I saw thrones, and they sat upon them, and judgment was given unto them: and I saw the souls of them that were beheaded for the witness of Jesus, and for the Word of God, and which had not worshipped the Beast, neither his image, neither had received his mark upon their foreheads, or in their hands; and they lived and reigned with Christ a thousand years. But the rest of the dead lived not again until the thousand years were finished. This is the first resurrection. Blessed and holy is he that hath part in the first resurrection: on such the second death hath no power, but they shall be priests of God and of Christ, and shall reign with Him a thousand years. And when the thousand years are expired, Satan shall be loosed out of his prison, And shall go out to deceive the nations which are in the four quarters of the earth, Gog and Magog, to gather them together to battle: the number of whom is as the sand of the sea. And they went up on the breadth of the earth, and compassed the camp of the saints about, and the beloved city: and fire came down from God out of heaven, and devoured them. And the devil that deceived them was cast into the lake of fire and brimstone, where the Beast and the False Prophet are, and shall be tormented day and night for ever and ever. And I saw a great white throne, and Him that sat on it, from Whose face the earth and the heaven fled away; and there was found no place for them. And I saw the dead, small and great, stand before God; and the books were opened: and another book was opened, which is the book of life: and the dead were judged out of those things which were written in the books, according to their works. And the sea gave up the dead which were in it; and death and hell delivered up the dead which were in them: and they were judged every man according to their works. And death and hell were cast into the lake of fire. This is the second death. And whosoever was not found written in the book of life was cast into the lake of fire.*

Notice the difference here between Satan and the Beast and False Prophet. Satan is held in reserve in the bottomless pit, where he awaits a temporary release after a thousand years, and then final judgement. The Beast and False Prophet are in the lake of fire for eternity. The thousand-year period we might interpret as fulfilling the remainder of the celebrations of the marriage, for this is the time of Israel's emergence as the people of God on the earth, the long awaited and prophetic period when they are in favour with God, and through whom the Lord rules the kingdoms of the earth. A percentage of the people who make up this new Israel are those who are resurrected to live again. We are not told how long they live for, but this seems to have been the hope of Martha, for example, when she said to the Lord (John 11:24): *I know that he shall rise again in the resurrection at the last day.*

At the end of this period Satan is released, and once again tries to deceive the nations, this time through the offices of [99]Gog and Magog, whose intention is to attack Israel, which by now is enjoying a [100]peaceful co-existence with its neighbours.

99. It is not absolutely clear who these nations are, but are North of Israel, possibly Russian.
100. Ezekiel 38.

This time it is God Himself Who intervenes on behalf of His nation Israel, and destroys the massed forces that are assembled. Many difficulties present themselves in scripture because of the two separate attempts of Satan to destroy Israel, firstly through Babylon, the Beast and False Prophet, and then one thousand years later through inciting the nations Gog and Magog. Confusion can follow if Old Testament prophecies are forced to conform to events to which they do not belong, and great care must be taken to *rightly divide the Word of truth* here, and allow scripture to interpret itself. There is much written about the blessings that will come on Israel in its final one thousand years, and many of the prophecies of the major and minor prophetic writings reach beyond the great tribulation, and are clearly yet to be fulfilled. Israel has never yet fulfilled its proper place as the people of God on earth, and this is yet to be seen.

It is a legitimate question to ask why Satan is released to stir up the nations against Israel after so long a time, and my own view is that this is the final trial for God's people, who now, as a nation, will prove themselves worthy of His investment in them. Now, trusting in God alone, and having no defence other than their submission to Him, they vindicate God and His Son's trust in them, and glorify Him through their sole reliance on Him when the forces of Gog and Magog are arrayed against them.

Finally they demonstrate the faith that He has always looked for, and He can close the chapter on Israel's trials. We next read of the final judgements of the earth, the great white throne, where the books are opened, and those not included are cast into the lake of fire, to join Satan, the Beast and the False Prophet. Death and hell themselves follow shortly after, presumably including the bottomless pit described earlier as the temporary abode of the dead. It is also at this time that the earth and the heavens are destroyed, fleeing from the face of the righteous judge.

CHAPTER TWELVE

NEW HEAVEN, NEW EARTH

❈

Revelation 21:1-4: *And I saw a new heaven and a new earth: for the first heaven and the first earth were passed away; and there was no more sea. And I John saw the holy city, new Jerusalem, coming down from God out of heaven, prepared as a bride adorned for her husband. And I heard a great voice out of heaven saying, Behold, the tabernacle of God is with men, and He will dwell with them, and they shall be His people, and God Himself shall be with them, and be their God. And God shall wipe away all tears from their eyes; and there shall be no more death, neither sorrow, nor crying, neither shall there be any more pain: for the former things are passed away.*

This is perhaps the most astounding news of all, that after all that has gone before, and God having made His point concerning the nation Israel, both the world that we know and the heaven that exists at present are destroyed. This is the true union and marriage of the Son to the bride, which is the New Jerusalem that God forms. Now is the time that God will dwell amongst His people for eternity, and obtain that which He always wanted, which is fellowship with His created beings, through His Son. This world reminds us of the former time of innocence in Eden, when there were fewer seas, no tears and no death, only fellowship with the Lord in the garden.

Revelation 21:5-8: *And He that sat upon the throne said, Behold, I make all things new. And He said unto me, Write: for these words are true and faithful. And He said unto me, It is done. I am Alpha and Omega, the beginning and the end. I will give unto him that is athirst of the fountain of the water of life freely. He that overcometh shall inherit all things; and I will be His God, and he shall be My son. But the fearful, and unbelieving, and the abominable, and murderers, and whoremongers, and sorcerers, and idolaters, and all liars, shall have their part in the lake which burneth with fire and brimstone: which is the second death.*

Having glimpsed the New Jerusalem, John is reminded that he must write these true and faithful words down which come from the [101]Alpha and Omega Himself. The promises are to the faithful, those who in so many cases have died for their faith. For these nothing is withheld, they will partake of eternal life to its fullest extent. Those who have fallen short, the fearful and unbelieving (timid, faithless), who have become a stink in God's nose because of their actions and refusal to acknowledge Him, have their part in the lake of fire, from where there is no return, described here as the second death. Returning to the narrative, John is given more information regarding the bride, the Lamb's wife:

Revelation 21:9-27: *And there came unto me one of the seven angels which had the seven vials full of the seven last plagues, and talked with me, saying, Come hither, I will shew thee the bride, the Lamb's wife. And he carried me away in the spirit to a great and high mountain, and shewed me that great city, the holy Jerusalem, descending out of heaven from God, Having the glory of God: and her light was like unto*

101. Alpha and Omega being, of course, the first and last letters of the Greek alphabet.

a stone most precious, even like a jasper stone, clear as crystal; And had a wall great and high, and had twelve gates, and at the gates twelve angels, and names written thereon, which are the names of the twelve tribes of the children of Israel: On the east three gates; on the north three gates; on the south three gates; and on the west three gates. And the wall of the city had twelve foundations, and in them the names of the twelve apostles of the Lamb.

And he that talked with me had a golden reed to measure the city, and the gates thereof, and the wall thereof. And the city lieth foursquare, and the length is as large as the breadth: and he measured the city with the reed, [102]twelve thousand furlongs. The length and the breadth and the height of it are equal. And he measured the wall thereof, an hundred and forty and four cubits, according to the measure of a man, that is, of the angel. And the building of the wall of it was of jasper: and the city was pure gold, like unto clear glass. And the foundations of the wall of the city were garnished with all manner of precious stones. The first foundation was jasper; the second, sapphire; the third, a chalcedony; the fourth, an emerald; The fifth, sardonyx; the sixth, sardius; the seventh, chrysolite; the eighth, beryl; the ninth, a topaz; the tenth, a chrysoprasus; the eleventh, a jacinth; the twelfth, an amethyst. And the twelve gates were twelve pearls; every several gate was of one pearl: and the street of the city was pure gold, as it were transparent glass.

And I saw no temple therein: for the Lord God Almighty and the Lamb are the temple of it. And the city had no need of the sun, neither of the moon, to shine in it: for the glory of God did lighten it, and the Lamb is the light thereof. And the nations of them which are saved shall walk in the light of it: and the kings of the earth do bring their glory and honour into it. And the gates of it shall not be shut at all by day: for there shall be no night there. And they shall bring the glory and

---

102. A furlong is about 202 English yards, making this measurement around 1377 miles. The wall is approximately 300 yards high, so either there is a mistake in the writing and this is not a perfect cube, or the city is set on the 'great and high mountain', making it the same height as the length, which seems unlikely, as access would be difficult.

honour of the nations into it. And there shall in no wise enter into it any thing that defileth, neither whatsoever worketh abomination, or maketh a lie: but they which are written in the Lamb's book of life.

There is nothing that can be added to the wonderful description of these things except to emphasise that the city here, the New Jerusalem, owes nothing to the present day Gentile Church. Every reference is Jewish, and is the culmination of the promises made to that nation that their God would dwell amongst them. This was the purpose of the tabernacle in the wilderness, that their God was seen to be dwelling among them. This takes nothing away from the promises made to the believers of this present dispensation of grace the Gentile Church, for we are His body a part of Him, and so we go where He goes.

There is no need to appropriate to ourselves that which is clearly Jewish, neither should we feel hard done by, for at the end of the day, we are all the children of Abraham through faith. We can avoid a great deal of confusion by accepting the truth about whom these things were written to, and to whom they apply. Why try to read the Church into a place where it clearly does not belong? Why lessen the promises we already have in an attempt to grab all the limelight? It does not make sense to do it, and neither can we justify it by scripture. We should rightly divide these truths, as Paul taught us.

Revelation 22:1-5: *And he shewed me a pure river of water of life, clear as crystal, proceeding out of the throne of God and of the Lamb. In the midst of the street of it, and on either side of the river, was there the tree of life, which bare twelve manner of fruits, and yielded her fruit every month: and the leaves of the tree were for the [103]healing of the nations. And there shall be no more curse: but the throne of God and of the*

---

103. The Greek word used here is 'therapiea', a cure, from where we get our English word therapy.

Lamb shall be in it; and His servants shall serve Him: And they shall see His face; and His name shall be in their foreheads. And there shall be no night there; and they need no candle, neither light of the sun; for the Lord God giveth them light: and they shall reign for ever and ever.

Here we see the intended purpose of the tree of life, which was so jealously guarded after the fall in the Garden of Eden. Under the right circumstances, when God is in control, it can be used to yield the fruit intended for men, restoring and keeping them in their proper place in the Father's will, that is, [104]eternal life.

The danger in Eden was that the man would take the fruit of this tree before he was ready, for the tree of the knowledge of good and evil probably tempted Satan first, causing him to fall. He knew he had to try and prevent his own eventual death, and so corrupted the woman, to get at the man. The description of the Tree of Life, places it across the Water of Life and indicates that both the leaves and the fruit would drop into the waters which would then be available with those with the right to drink. This echoes the Lord's words in John about Himself and the Holy Spirit that He would send:

John 4:10-14: *Jesus answered and said unto her, If thou knewest the gift of God, and Who it is that saith to thee, Give Me to drink; thou wouldest have asked of Him, and He would have given thee living water. The woman saith unto Him, Sir, Thou hast nothing to draw with, and the well is deep: from whence then hast Thou that living water? Art Thou greater than our father Jacob, which gave us the well, and drank*

---

104. Genesis 3:22-23. Man had become corrupted, and death had been introduced through having eaten the fruit of the tree of the knowledge of good and evil. This did not bring the benefits that Satan had promised, to make them wise, and as gods, but rather was their downfall, introducing sin and death into their experience. The Lord hung on the 'tree' in Jerusalem, and so dealt with death by the cross, providing man with the possibility of once again enjoying fellowship with Himself and the Father in the garden of the New Jerusalem. There is no mention of the tree of the knowledge of good and evil in the New Jerusalem; on the contrary, there is no more death, and men can drink freely of the water of life!

thereof himself, and his children, and his cattle? Jesus answered and said unto her, Whosoever drinketh of this water shall thirst again: But whosoever drinketh of the water that I shall give him shall never thirst; but the water that I shall give him shall be in him a well of water springing up into everlasting life.

And we are reminded too

John 7:37-39: *In the last day, that great day of the feast, Jesus stood and cried, saying, If any man thirst, let him come unto Me, and drink. He that believeth on Me, as the scripture hath said, out of His belly shall flow rivers of living water. (But this spake He of the Spirit, which they that believe on Him should receive: for the Holy Ghost was not yet given; because that Jesus was not yet glorified.)*

There can be little doubt left that the "pure river of water of life" is nothing less than the Holy Spirit, the third person of the Trinity, still doing His work to glorify the Father and the Son.

Revelation 22:6-13: *And he said unto me, These sayings are faithful and true: and the Lord God of the holy prophets sent His angel to shew unto His servants the things which must shortly be done. Behold, I come quickly: blessed is he that keepeth the sayings of the prophecy of this book. And I John saw these things, and heard them. And when I had heard and seen, I fell down to worship before the feet of the angel which shewed me these things. Then saith he unto me, See thou do it not: for I am thy fellowservant, and of thy brethren the prophets, and of them which keep the sayings of this book: worship God. And he saith unto me, Seal not the sayings of the prophecy of this book: for the time is at hand. He that is unjust, let him be unjust still: and he which is filthy, let him be filthy still: and he that is righteous, let him be righteous still:*

and he that is holy, let him be holy still. And, behold, I come quickly;
and My reward is with Me, to give every man according as his work
shall be. I am Alpha and Omega, the beginning and the end, the first
and the last.

Returning to the narrative, we see that John returns to telling
of his falling down and worshipping the angel. In my view, it is
unlikely that John would have done this twice, having already
been told not to, so it is more likely that he is repeating the fact
that he was so overwhelmed by the truth of what he saw that
he felt compelled to worship. Again the blessing contained in
this book, this revealing of the perfect will of God, is seen to be
for all the world, and even as John was writing it, the time was
considered to be at hand. How much nearer are we to these
events happening than John was, nearly two thousand years ago!

Interestingly, there is no requirement for John to try and
preach or push his book onto others; he was just to write it and
send it to the seven churches, and it would do its work from
there – which it did. Those that despise the Book of Revelation,
and other prophecies concerning the End Times, are free to
carry on with whatever it is that is so important to them. It does
not alter the fact that the Lord is preparing to come, and in His
Father's time, all of those things given to Him in the Revelation
will be fulfilled, perhaps not as we think they will be, but
nevertheless, exactly as they are written.

John seems to break off here, to refer again to the blessing
prepared for those willing to alter their lives to please God, and
to whom is a sure reward. Not so for them that are 'without,'
and not prepared to change, for these shall not get close to such
blessing. Clearly the choice is the individual man's to make.
Once the information has been made available, he alone bears
responsibility for his actions.

Revelation 22:14-19: *"Blessed are they that do His commandments, that they may have right to the tree of life, and may enter in through the gates into the city. For without are dogs, and sorcerers, and whoremongers, and murderers, and idolaters, and whosoever loveth and maketh a lie. I Jesus have sent mine angel to testify unto you these things in the churches. I am the root and the offspring of David, and the bright and morning star. And the Spirit and the bride say, Come. And let him that heareth say, Come. And let him that is athirst come. And whosoever will, let him take the water of life freely. For I testify unto every man that heareth the words of the prophecy of this book, If any man shall add unto these things, God shall add unto him the plagues that are written in this book: And if any man shall take away from the words of the book of this prophecy, God shall take away his part out of the book of life, and out of the holy city, and from the things which are written in this book.*

The testimony here is to those that hear the word of the prophecy, and so these words must be a comfort to them in the light of the world's continual effort to deny or modify parts of it, by altering the revelation given, or by adding to it what is not there. Presumably, those that seek the truths contained within the book are not in this category, as the study of the book is encouraged, to obtain the blessing it contains.

The last word here surely belongs to the Lord, Who is the last word on everything, the *Alpha and Omega* Himself. A better translation here is: *"YES, I COME QUICKLY"* as if to answer for us the burning question we are about to ask.

Revelation 22:20-21: *He which testifieth these things saith, Surely I come quickly. Amen. Even so, come, Lord Jesus. The grace of our Lord Jesus Christ be with you all. Amen.*

www.ingramcontent.com/pod-product-compliance
Lightning Source LLC
LaVergne TN
LVHW051729080426
835511LV00018B/2950